Public Record Office Readers' Guide No 16

D1466058

NEW TO KEW?

a first time guide for family historians
at the Public Record Office, Kew

Jane Cox

PRO Publications

**For all those who have Bethnal
Green ancestry, with love.**

ACKNOWLEDGEMENTS

I must thank Susan Lumas née Grover, Mark Dunton and Simon Fowler, for answering all my idiot questions, my son, Oliver Hoare, for sorting out the word processor for me, Charles Teviot for giving me the first words of genealogical advice I ever received (which bus to take to get to St Anne's Limehouse), Trevor Chalmers and Melvyn Stainton for the drawings, Millie Skinns for designing the book and Julia Wigg for sorting everything out.

PRO Publications
Public Record Office
Ruskin Avenue
Kew
Surrey
TW9 4DU

© Crown Copyright 1997

ISBN 1 873162 40 5

A catalogue card for this book is available from the British Library.

CONTENTS

ILLUSTRATIONS

Front cover photograph by John Critchley

PART I

Introduction

ABOUT THIS BOOK

This guide deals with the prime sources for family history in the Public Record Office (PRO) at Kew; there are many more as you will discover as you get acquainted with the place. It replaces the popular Reader's Guide No. 4 *Never Been Here Before?* but deals only with the records held at Kew. A new version of *Never Been Here Before?* with the same title but dealing only with records seen at the new Family Records Centre in Myddelton Street, which was opened in March 1997, will be published in August 1997.

The Public Record Office is the national archive for England and Wales; the records are those of the central government and law courts and span 900 years, starting with Domesday Book.

Some of the most popular sources for family history have been microfilmed and may be consulted, along with indexes to centrally registered birth, marriage and death records (Office for National Statistics: General Register Office) at the Family Records Centre in Myddelton Street in central London (see pp 3-5).

There is, however, a whole range of records at PRO Kew which family historians find of immense use in tracking down ancestors and for filling in details about their lives. This guide is intended for the newcomer and the reader in a hurry. It tells you how to work the system and provides a step-by-step guide to researching the prime sources.

For a more detailed description of the PRO's genealogical holdings see *Tracing your Ancestors in the Public Record Office* (revised edition, HMSO, 1992).

For those of you who have access to the Internet, the World Wide Web address of the PRO site is http://www.open.gov.uk/pro/prohome.htm

Should you be at Kew or the Family Records Centre?

The starting point for English and Welsh family history in London is the Family Records Centre, where you can trace your family back perhaps several hundreds of years - maybe more - using the PRO's prime genealogical sources, the General Register Office's birth, marriage and death records and the Mormon index of parish registers and other sources (the International Genealogical Index or IGI).

A comprehensive catalogue of the records in the PRO is the *Public Record Office Guide* which can be consulted in the Research Enquiries Room. You can buy a microfiche copy of the 1996 edition in the shop. This publication is not designed for family historians and you will probably not have recourse to it until you are quite experienced.

Reading this guide may save you time.

The Family Records Centre holds:

PRO sources on film or fiche:
- census returns 1841, 1851, 1861, 1871, 1881, 1891.
- Nonconformist chapel registers, seventeenth century to nineteenth century, main series (some also at Kew, see p 92).
- wills, fourteenth century to 1858, some, namely those proved in the Prerogative Court of Canterbury (PCC) only.
- Death Duty records 1796 to 1858 (records 1858-1904 can be read in the original at Kew, see p 59).

General Register Office (formerly in St. Catherine's House. Certificates have to be bought as before.)

• Indexes to the civil registers of births, marriage and death records from 1837.

The Mormon (LDS) name index to parish registers and other sources (IGI) and the Mormon Family Search CD-Rom programme

For a description of the records and workings of the centre see the forthcoming companion volume to this guide, *Never been here before? A first time guide to the Family Records Centre* which will be published in August 1997.

How to get to Kew

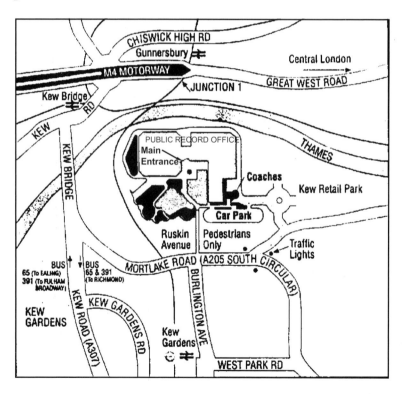

Public Record Office, Ruskin Avenue, Kew, Richmond, Surrey TW9 4DU. Tel: 0181 876 3444; enquiries 0181 392 5261. To order documents in advance ring 0181 392 5261. You will need exact references and your reader's ticket number if you have one.

Opening hours: 9.30 am to 5 pm Monday, Wednesday, Friday and (from 5 July 1997) Saturday; 10 am to 7 pm Tuesday; 9.30 am to 7 pm Thursday.

How to get to Myddelton Street

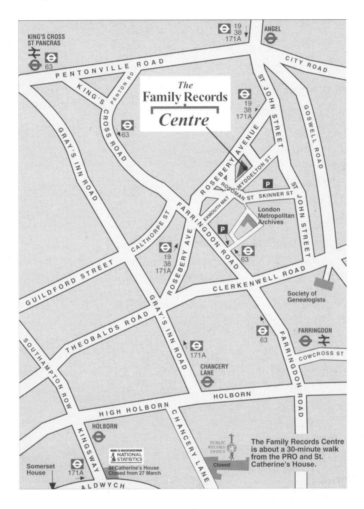

Family Records Centre, 1 Myddelton Street, London EC1R 1UW. Tel: 0181 392 5300.

Opening hours: 9 am to 5 pm Monday, Wednesday and Friday; 10 am to 7 pm Tuesday; 9 am to 7 pm Thursday; 9.30 am to 5 pm Saturday.

Vital sources elsewhere

Records of Scots and Irish Ancestors

Scots

The Family Records Centre has the
Scottish Link, a computer database of
indexes to records held at the Scottish Register Office in Edinburgh. For a
moderate fee (£4 per half hour at May 1997) you can search the database. The
indexes cover:

- births, marriages and deaths 1855 to date
- divorce files 1984 to date
- old parish registers 1553-1854
- 1891 census returns (a name index)

Copies of the records themselves can be ordered (for a further fee) from the
General Register Office at New Register House, 3 West Street, Edinburgh EH1
3YT.

Records of the many Scots who served in the British Army, Royal Navy and
Merchant Navy are in PRO Kew (see pp 28, 87 and 104). You may find it useful
to buy one of the guides to tracing Scottish ancestry available in the PRO shop.

Irish

Many of the records you need for Irish family history are in Ireland. Buy one of
the guides to Irish genealogy in the PRO shop.

For birth, marriage and death records for the whole of Ireland from 1864 (non-
Roman Catholic marriages from 1845) until 1921, and for Eire to date, apply to
the General Register Office of Ireland, Joyce House, 8-11 Lombard Street, Dublin
2, Ireland. Tel: 003531 6711863. Indexes are held in LDS (Mormon) Family
History Centres.

Records of births, marriages and deaths in Northern Ireland from 1 January 1922 are with the Registrar General in Belfast at the General Register Office (Northern Ireland), Oxford House, Chichester Street, Belfast BT1 4HL. Tel: 01232 235211.

Census returns and other records are held in the National Archives of Ireland, Bishop Street, Dublin 8. Tel: 003531 478 3711. The 1901 and 1911 censuses have been filmed and the films may be ordered from Salt Lake City and read at LDS (Mormon) Family History Centres.

The service records of men who served in the Royal Irish Constabulary are at PRO Kew (see p 95), as are the records of Irishmen who served in the British Army and Royal Navy (see pp 28 and 104).

Wills from 1858 (England and Wales)

Wills proved from January 1858 to date can be read at the Principal Registry of the Family Division, Somerset House, Strand, London WC2R 1LP. Tel: 0171 936 6948/6569. The office is open between 10 am and 4.30 pm Monday to Friday. There are plans for relocation, so ring and check before you go.

Copies can be ordered by post for a small fee if you have an approximate date of death. Write to the Chief Clerk, York Probate Sub-Registry, Duncombe Place, York YO1 2EA.

Parish registers (England and Wales) for pre-1837 births, marriages and deaths

From the sixteenth century the Church of England has kept registers of baptisms, marriages and burials. From the seventeenth century, in addition, there were Nonconformist chapels where registers were kept. The data in these records are the family historian's chief building blocks for the period before national registration was introduced (1837).

Most parish (Church of England) registers are now in local record offices. To locate the ones you want, consult the *Phillimore Atlas and Index of Parish Registers* (C R Humphrey Smith, Chichester, 2nd ed 1995) and J S W Gibson's *Record Offices: How to Find Them* (Federation of Family History Societies, 1996). Both are available in the Research Enquiries Room and can be bought in the PRO bookshop. Always check by telephoning or writing to the record office or library in question, to avoid wasted journeys.

Many chapel registers are at the Family Records Centre, some are at PRO Kew (see p 92), and some are held locally.

A number of Welsh registers are held in the National Library of Wales.

Until the nineteenth century the vast majority of people in England came under the auspices of the Church of England, so the chances are you will have to go to a local record office to find your family.

The International Genealogical Index (IGI)

While you are at PRO Kew you can use the Mormon index (IGI). This fiche index (in the Microfilm Reading Room) has many thousands of entries of baptisms and some marriages from parish and Nonconformist registers and other sources. It is the most valuable of research tools, but should be treated with care as there are many errors and omissions. Always follow up your research in the IGI by going to the original registers.

The IGI is widely available in local history libraries, Mormon (LDS) Family History Centres, etc. There is a copy at the Family Records Centre in Myddelton Street.

The Society of Genealogists, the Federation of Family History Societies, LDS (Mormon) Family History Centres and the FamilySearch CD-ROM programme

Anyone embarking on family history should know about these organizations.

The Society of Genealogists at 14 Charterhouse Buildings, London EC1M 7BA (tel: 0171 251 8799), has a library of published and unpublished indexes and reference works which are of immense value to family historians; many are mentioned in this book. You can either join the library by paying a fee or research there, paying on a daily or half daily basis.

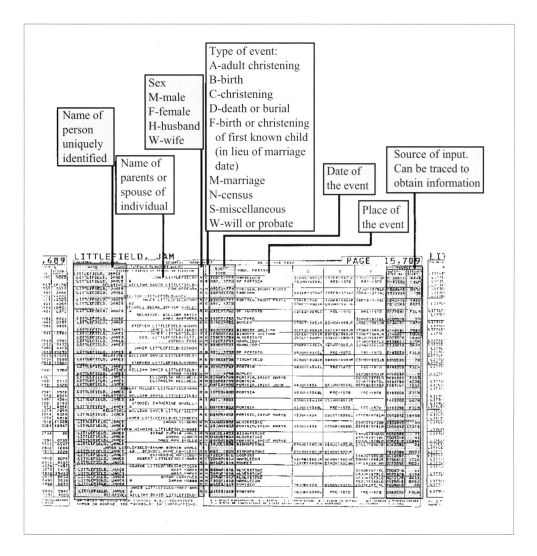

The Mormon Parish Register or International Genealogical Index (IGI)
(reproduced by kind permission of the
Church of Jesus Christ of Latter-Day Saints)

The Federation of Family History Societies at the Benson Room, Birmingham and Midland Institute, Margaret Street, Birmingham B3 3BS, co-ordinates the large number of local family history societies which now exist. These societies meet regularly and publish journals. You can join the society nearest to home or local to the place of your family roots - both if you like! They provide moral support, information and a lot of fun. Write to the Federation with an s.a.e. for more information. Many of their record guides are sold in the PRO shop.

The Mormon Church (Church of Jesus Christ of Latter-Day Saints, or LDS) has filmed and indexed vast runs of records vital to the pursuit of family history worldwide. At Mormon Family History centres throughout the country you can consult these films. Most have to be ordered from the LDS headquarters at Utah in Salt Lake City and may take a month to come. A small fee is charged for these films. For those who cannot spend time and money travelling around this is a good way to do family research. Look up your local Family History Centre in the telephone book or ask in your local library.

Most Family History Centres have the CD-ROM *FamilySearch*, a computerized version of the IGI. It also includes other genealogical data from worldwide sources. For the pre-1837 search this is a vital tool, having data from parish registers and other (LDS Church) sources. Playing around with this may achieve more in half an hour than years of conventional research! The CD-ROM is also available at the Family Records Centre, the Society of Genealogists and the Guildhall Library, Aldermanbury London EC2P 2EJ.

PART II

Using PRO Kew

USING PRO KEW

To research in the public records you will need a reader's ticket: this gives access to the research area and is also used for ordering records.

Keep your ticket with you all the time you are in the PRO.

Make sure you have some formal means of identification

- cheque guarantee card
- driving licence

If you are not a UK citizen you must show

- your passport
- national I D card

Children under fourteen must be accompanied by an adult who holds a reader's ticket. The adult has to sign a declaration taking responsibility for the child. Children of fourteen plus may be issued with their own ticket.

You will need to bring

A pound coin (refundable) for
the luggage lockers

Paper

PENCILS ONLY, PLEASE

A pencil

You may take only six loose sheets of paper into the research area but a notebook is O.K.

- there is no charge for doing your own research
- there is no need to book
- most of the records relate to England and Wales
- you can buy copies of most records
- in most cases records are not available until they are thirty years old
- some sensitive records are kept closed for longer.

The Building

Ground Floor

There is a reception desk in the entrance hall where reader's tickets are issued and general enquiries dealt with, a bookshop, a restaurant, telephones, cloakrooms, toilets and an exhibition area.

To get into the research area (the first and second floors) you must pass through a security point using your reader's ticket (swipe card).

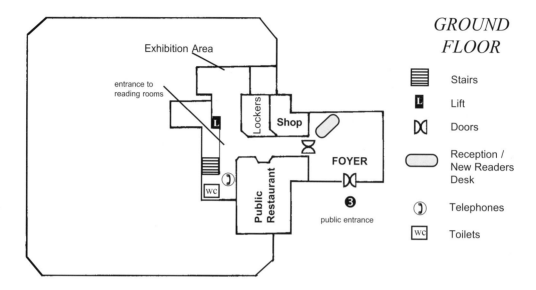

First Floor

There is a Document Reading Room (where all original records are read unless they are maps or very large) and a Microfilm Reading Room.

In between these two large rooms there is a Research Enquiries Room and lobby where catalogues and indexes are kept. There are 'help desks' and a video which tells you about the PRO. Reference works are kept on the shelves in the Research Enquiries Room, the Microfilm Reading Room and the PRO's library, which is at the far end of the Microfilm Reading Room. Books may be requested from the library catalogue and either read in the library or taken into the reading rooms. Certain material is available for browsing on the open shelves, namely, annuals, records related books, calendars, periodicals and topographical works. There is a photocopy shop at the far end of the Document Reading Room.

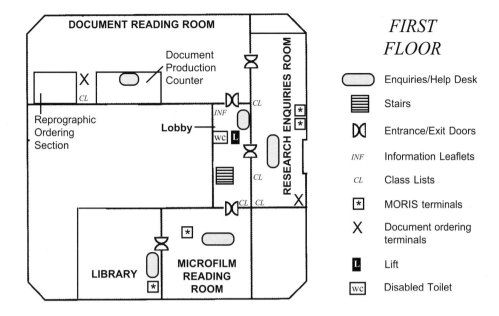

FIRST FLOOR

DOCUMENT READING ROOM

Document Production Counter

RESEARCH ENQUIRIES ROOM

Reprographic Ordering Section

Lobby

LIBRARY

MICROFILM READING ROOM

⬭	Enquiries/Help Desk
▤	Stairs
⋈	Entrance/Exit Doors
INF	Information Leaflets
CL	Class Lists
✳	MORIS terminals
X	Document ordering terminals
L	Lift
wc	Disabled Toilet

Second Floor

The public area on the second floor is one large room where maps and large documents are produced. There is also a photocopy shop.

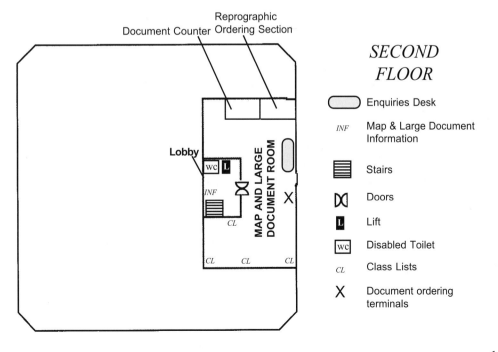

Document Counter   Reprographic Ordering Section

SECOND FLOOR

Lobby

MAP AND LARGE DOCUMENT ROOM

⬭	Enquiries Desk
INF	Map & Large Document Information
▤	Stairs
⋈	Doors
L	Lift
wc	Disabled Toilet
CL	Class Lists
X	Document ordering terminals

Planning your day at Kew

PRO Kew is nowhere near any other family history centre and it is a fair step to any shops, restaurants or pubs. Once you have arrived in the building, it is as well to stay until closing time and make the most of the in-house facilities.

Food and drink

There is a restaurant on the ground floor which is open from 9 am to 3.50 pm on Monday, Wednesday and Friday, and until 5.30 pm on Tuesday and Thursday, serving breakfast from 9 am to 11 am and lunch from 11.30 am to 2 pm. From 5 July 1997 it will also be open on Saturday from 10.30 am to 2.30 pm for light snacks. If you bring sandwiches, you can eat them in the restaurant or outside on the grass if it is fine.

Toilets

The toilets are on the ground floor; there are none in the research areas.

Telephones

There are pay phones in the foyer on the ground floor, taking both coins and phone cards (available from the shop).

Disabled readers

Lifts and disabled toilets are available.

The bookshop

The shop sells a wide range of general family history guides, guides to PRO records, books of general historical and military interest, PRO souvenirs, postcards, greeting cards, pencils and paper. Books can be ordered by post; add 20% for postage and packing.

Exhibition Area

Temporary exhibitions of facsimile records are mounted here.

Equipment you need

You will need a notebook. Only six loose sheets of paper are allowed into the research area, so it is best to have some that are bound together. You will need pencils or a word processor/typewriter, as you are not allowed to write with pens or biros in the research area. Electrical sockets are available in a designated area for readers with laptop computers.

Making the most of your time

Unless the records you want are on film you will have to order them and there may be a waiting time of half an hour or more. Use this time to browse around, looking at books and indexes on the bookshelves. You never know what you might find.

With long, complicated records, it is a good idea to buy a copy to save yourself long hours of transcription. Most records can be copied on the spot, so you can take the copy home with you and struggle with it at your leisure.

What do I do first?

Step 1   Get a reader's ticket from the desk in the entrance hall

The reader's ticket is a swipe card which gives you access to the research area; you will also need it to order documents on the computer. It lasts for several years and is renewable.

You will need to show some formal means of identification, such as a bank card or driving licence. If you are not a UK citizen you will need to show your passport or national ID card.

Step 2   Look at the list of records on page 18 and decide which you want to research. Then turn to the relevant pages of this guide.

You can sit in the foyer or restaurant while you do this.

Step 3   **Deposit your coat and briefcase/handbag** in the cloakroom and go up to the research area.

You will need a pound coin to open a locker where you will have to leave your belongings. It will be returned when you retrieve them. ***Make a note of the*** *locker's number; it is not on the key*. Take with you your reader's ticket, pencil/ PC, notebook and money (for photocopies) and anything else you might need (angina pills, spectacles, magnifying glass, a copy of this guide).

Now go through the security point using your reader's ticket/swipe card - and upstairs to the research area.

Step 4 Finding the reference numbers for the records you want to research.

Each of the record sections in this guide explains the procedure for identifying and ordering the sources it describes. If you get stuck go to the nearest enquiry desk.

For each subject covered in this guide there is a free information leaflet which you will find in the pigeon holes in the lobby on the first floor.

Every item, whether it be a register, file or loose paper, has its own unique reference number. You will need this number to order it.

The reference is made up of a lettercode and two numbers (usually). The lettercode denotes the government department or law court where the records originated; thus ADM for Admiralty, E for Exchequer etc. The number following is the 'class' number and denotes a category of records; thus ADM 36 is Ships' Muster Books. The next number identifies the individual item, which is referred to as a 'piece' in the PRO. ADM 36/54, for example, is the muster book for HMS *Aldborough* from January to June 1737. For some items you may also need a sub-number, e.g. E 179/160/231.

To find the particular file/register/paper you need for your research you must consult the catalogues (called 'class lists' in the PRO) which you will find in binders on the open shelves. There are sets of these, in the lobby, Research Enquiries Room, Document Reading Room and Map and Large Document Room. Class lists relating to records on film are kept in the Microfilm Reading Room. The catalogues are arranged according to their 'lettercode' and then by numbered classes of records.

Find the binder which contains your class list eg WO 97 or ADM 36. Look through it until you find the item you need and note the number which is in the left hand margin (there is a date and a description of each item on the right).

ADM 1	AN 2-6	BT 25	CO 4	DO 13	FO 6-9	HO 14	J 6	LCO 5

PRO 16	RG 12	RAIL 44	STAT 11	T 100	WO 97	WO 100	ZHC 17	ZPER 8

The reference number for your document will have three parts, eg WO 97/2000 or ADM 36/54. Once you have got this you are ready to order your document.

MORIS

MORIS stands for Means of Reference Information System. There are five computer terminals available for public use: two in the Research Enquiries Room, one in the Microfilm Reading Room, one in the Map and Large Document Reading Room, and one in the Library. MORIS will tell you what indexes and other means of reference there are to the different record classes - but you have to know which class of records you want before you interrogate him!

Thus, having found out from this book that WO 97 is the class number for soldiers' documents, key WO 97 into MORIS and he will list for you all the different sorts of indexes that are available in the PRO. He will not tell you of the existence of any indexes or other means of reference which may exist outside the PRO. MORIS will also tell you where the means of reference are, which room they are in and (if printed) what their Dewey decimal classification number is.

If you know the name of a reference work, key the title into MORIS and he will tell you whereabouts you can find it, provided, of course, that it is available in the PRO. You can also use MORIS for author and county searches.

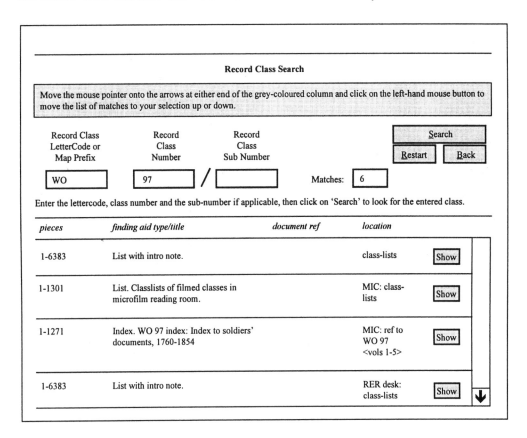

Record Class Search

Move the mouse pointer onto the arrows at either end of the grey-coloured column and click on the left-hand mouse button to move the list of matches to your selection up or down.

Record Class LetterCode or Map Prefix	Record Class Number	Record Class Sub Number		
			Search	
			Restart	Back
WO	97	/	Matches:	6

Enter the lettercode, class number and the sub-number if applicable, then click on 'Search' to look for the entered class.

pieces	finding aid type/title	document ref	location	
1-6383	List with intro note.		class-lists	Show
1-1301	List. Classlists of filmed classes in microfilm reading room.		MIC: class-lists	Show
1-1271	Index. WO 97 index: Index to soldiers' documents, 1760-1854		MIC: ref to WO 97 <vols 1-5>	Show
1-6383	List with intro note.		RER desk: class-lists	Show

Step 5   Get a bleeper and a seat

Before you order any records you need to get a 'bleeper' (pager) from the long counter in the Document Reading Room. The bleeper is a paging device which bleeps to tell you when your document has arrived. It has a number which corresponds to a seat in the Document Reading Room. This is your seat number for the day. Make a note of it, as you will need it when ordering records. You must not take this bleeper out of the building. Doing so will trigger an alarm.

Step 6   Ordering your record on the computer

There are document ordering computer terminals in the Research Enquiries Room. the Document Reading Room, the Microfilm Reading Room and the Map and Large Document Reading Room. Don't confuse them with the MORIS terminals.

Swipe your reader's ticket through the slot and key in your seat/bleeper number. Following the instructions given to you on screen key in the document reference, eg WO 97/542. You may order only three items at a time.

```
PDO01                RECORDS INFORMATION SYSTEM          12-MAY-97
                         Place Document Order
 ─────────────────────────────────────────────────────────────────

         Reader  1234567      N E       BODY      Location    64B


     Lettercode or      Class              Piece Number or        To (end
     Map Prefix         Number/Sub-No      Map Number             range)
      WO                 97  /              542                 -


     A copy of the document which you asked for is available in the Microfilm
     Reading Room.






 ──────────────────────────────────────────────────────────────────

 Count: *0                                              <Replace>
```

If the computer tells you that your record is on film go into the Microfilm Reading Room and help yourself to the film from the cabinets. The films are arranged in class code order. You can sit anywhere you like in this room, but make sure you take the numbered box next to your microfilm reader and put it in the place of the film you have removed from the cabinet.

Likewise, if your record is on microfiche, help yourself to the relevant fiche from the cabinet, remembering to put the numbered red card from the fiche reader in its place in the cabinet.

If the computer tells you that your record is 'available in the Research Enquiries Room', then ask at the enquiry desk whereabouts on the shelves it is.

If the computer simply tells you that your document has been ordered, then wait (about thirty minutes) until the bleeper bleeps to tell you it has arrived. You can go and have a cup of coffee downstairs, or browse around in the shop - the bleeper will reach you there.

When the bleeper goes off, go and collect your record from the long counter in the Document Reading Room. You will have to tell the staff what your seat number is. You can only have one record at a time, unless they are bound volumes. If want to read a number of items, make sure you order three more as soon as the first three have been delivered to the long counter.

If the computer tells you that your records are to be read in the Map and Large Document Room, then, when your bleeper goes off, go upstairs to the second floor and ask for your document at the counter there, giving your name.

If any complication arises about the documents you have ordered, go to the help desk opposite the long counter in the Document Reading Room.

HELP!

- The computer screen tells me that my reference doesn't work.
- The computer screen tells me that I can't have the record.

Ask at the help desk in the Document Reading Room or the Research Enquiries Room.

Step 7   Getting information from the records

You can, of course, take notes in pencil, or using a typewriter, word processor or dictaphone. Alternatively, or in addition, you can have copies made.

If you have problems understanding the documents - handwriting may be difficult and you will encounter unfamiliar terms - there are several courses of action. There is a range of inexpensive guides to help you understand the records, which you can buy in the shop. Staff will help you read the odd word or explain some archaic administrative term. If you are at a complete loss you might care to employ a professional researcher to help you. Ask for a list of names at an enquiry desk.

Step 8   Buying copies of the records

Most records may be photocopied on the spot. The PRO also offers very high quality colour copies which look as good as the documents themselves; this service takes about a week.

You can make your own copies of records which are on film or fiche; ask at the enquiry desk in the Microfilm Reading Room for a copier card and assistance in working the reader printer, if you get stuck.

Even records which are too fragile to be photocopied can usually be copied in some way or other. The PRO offers a wide range of reprographic services; there are photocopy shops in the Document Reading Room and in the Map and Large Document Room.

PART III

The Records A to Z

APPRENTICES

1710-1811

The Apprenticeship Books in the PRO (registers of tax paid on apprenticeship indentures) provide countrywide indexed lists of working men and women employed in a variety of trades.

On the shelves in the Research Enquiries Room are the indexes to the Apprenticeship Books (reference IR 17). The Books themselves bear the reference IR 1. The indexes are by master 1710 to 1762 and by apprentice 1710 to 1774 - so they do not cover the whole of IR 1.

Once you have found your entry in the indexes consult the catalogue labelled IR 1 and find the reference number for the Book you need. The Books are in two series: 'City' (tax paid in London) and 'Country' (tax paid elsewhere). You will need a three-part reference eg IR 1/45. Order it on the computer.

What information will I find?

Entries give the names, addresses and trades of the masters, the names of the apprentices and, until 1752, the names of their fathers (mothers if fathers were dead). Apprenticeships were normally served for seven years.

I know my ancestor worked as a shipwright, draper, carpenter, mason... why is he/she not there?

His/her apprenticeship may have been paid for by the Overseers of the Poor. There was no tax on these apprenticeships so they do not appear in the books. Many 'poor' apprentices were cheap labour for the local farmer - boys worked as agricultural labourers and girls as household servants.

The PRO series contains few entries for city or borough apprentices. For these go to the borough records which are held locally; those of London and Bristol are particularly full.

Your ancestor may never have served a formal apprenticeship - perhaps it was served within the family and no formal indenture was drawn up.

Your ancestor may have worked in a cotton mill or pursued some other occupation not in existence when the 1563 Statute of Apprentices was passed.

Other apprenticeship records in the PRO

Merchant naval apprentices, 1824-1953 (indexes) (reference BT 150 - BT 153)

Seamen's children. Registers of child apprentices from the Royal Naval School (Greenwich Hospital School), 1728-1838 (reference ADM 73/421-448)

Soldiers' children. Admission and Discharge registers for the Royal Military Asylum (later Duke of York's Military School) 1803-1923 (reference WO 143/ 17-26).

ARMY SERVICE RECORDS

Seventeenth century to the First World War

Before starting your research find out, if you can, your ancestor's regiment or a campaign in which he fought. This will make your research easier.

There is a wide range of sources for military genealogy. You would be well advised to buy:

Army Records for Family Historians (Simon Fowler, PRO Readers' Guide No. 2, 1992, £4.75)

Army Service Records of the First World War (Simon Fowler et al, PRO, 1996, £5.99)

Both are available in the bookshop and can be consulted in the Microfilm Reading Room and Research Enquiries Room.

What information will I get from the records?

This varies from period to period. There are regular records from the 1660s but the most fruitful searches are likely to be from the mid-eighteenth century to the 1920s.

1.   *His career*

Whether your ancestor was a private or an officer, you should be able to trace his progress through the army: his promotions, punishments, medals, wounds, discharge and pension, or death. You can find out where he was stationed and which battles he fought in. Was he really at Waterloo, or is that a family story which grew up, based on an old soldier's boasting?

Before 1871 soldiers enlisted for a twenty-one year period and usually served until they were disabled by wounds or old age. From 1871 they could opt for a twelve-year short service engagement. Officers bought their commissions (until 1871) and sold them when they wished to retire.

Was he really at Waterloo?

2.   *What he looked like*

The Army needed to know what soldiers looked like for identification purposes. There may be a description of your great-grandfather telling you that he was six foot tall, had fair hair, blue eyes and a tattoo on his chest! These descriptions are to be found among personal service records and some pension records.

The Imperial War Museum's Photographic Archive (All Saints' Annexe, Austal Street, London SE11, near Lambeth North Underground station) has millions of First World War and Second World War photographs. If you know your father's or grandfather's unit, it is worth a search. Regimental museums also have photographs.

3.   *Family details*

You should be able to find his birth date, year and place, and information about his marriage and death if he died in service. There may also be details of his children and his trade before he entered the Army.

Records of regular soldiers ('other ranks')

'Other ranks' includes privates in the infantry, troopers in the cavalry, trumpeters and drummers, corporals and sergeants.

Which regiment was he in?

The army was divided into regiments and corps (Royal Artillery and Royal Engineers), composed of between 600 and 1,000 men. Each regiment was divided into battalions and then companies. It will help you to know your ancestor's regiment, as many of the records are arranged by regiment. Also, the British Army was a huge fighting force and there were many soldiers with the same name. Knowing the regiment will help you to distinguish your Private John Archer from all the others with the same name.

If you know where your ancestor came from and the rough dates he served in the Army it may be worth checking the lists of his local regiments. If John Archer came from Dorchester, for instance, he could perhaps have joined the Dorsetshire Regiment.

Finding his regiment (and something about him) from PRO sources

Soldiers discharged to pension 1760 to c. 1920:

1760-1854: check the name indexes to discharge papers (WO 97) on the bookshelves in the Microfilm Reading Room. There is also an on-line database of the names in this part of WO 97.

1855-1882: the documents are not arranged alphabetically by name (see page 33), so you would not be able to discover your soldier's regiment by this means.

1883-1913: the discharge papers themselves are arranged alphabetically for the whole army. Consult the catalogue labelled WO 97; it is divided into two sections. Find the item (piece) which includes the right part of the alphabet - if your soldier was called John Paxton, for instance, his discharge papers will be in WO97/3626 which has the papers for soldiers PAV to PAY. Order this on the computer and wait for your bleeper to tell you it has come. Collect it and search through the papers to see if he is there.

1914-c.1920: some of the service records for the First World War are in the PRO (see p 39) - there is about a one in ten chance of finding your soldier. Go to the binder labelled WO 364 in the Microfilm Reading Room. The arrangement is alphabetical. Find the item which may include your soldier and help yourself to the film from the cabinet. Wind on and see if your soldier is there.

Soldiers who died in service, 1810-1822, 1830-1844, 1862-1881:

Check the list of 'soldiers' effects' in the binder labelled WO 25 in the lobby or Research Enquiries Room. Some are arranged alphabetically by name, some numerically but with indexes. Order the appropriate record and see what it says about your soldier.

Soldiers in receipt of pensions, 1842-1862 (England and Scotland), 1842-1882 (Ireland):

Check the list of pensions in the binder labelled WO 22 in the lobby or Research Enquiries Room. You will need to know where your soldier lived when he was in retirement as the arrangement is alphabetical within area. Order the appropriate records and search for your soldier.

Soldiers in receipt of campaign medals from the First World War (most were):

Check the microfiche index of medal rolls in the cabinets in the middle of the Microfilm Reading Room. (See p 38 for more about medal rolls.)

You have a photograph of him in uniform:

Take it to the desk in the Research Enquiries Room; there are books which may help to identify his regiment from his uniform.

You know of a battle/campaign in which he fought:

Ask to see *In Search of the Forlorn Hope*, J M Kitzmiller (Utah, 1988). This book is kept behind the desk in the Research Enquiries Room and covers the period 1640 to the First World War. It is very useful but not completely reliable. It tells you which regiments fought in which campaigns/battles and you can then look at the Muster Rolls and Pay Lists (see p 36) for the units at the battle and see if your ancestor was there.

For important battles like Waterloo and the Somme there may be published lists. Ask.

Finding his regiment at the Family Records Centre, Myddelton Street

The GRO's Regimental Registers have alphabetical indexes to children born of serving men, soldiers 1716-1924.

Death certificates of soldiers (GRO) may give regiments.

Census returns (PRO) may give regiments. The 1881 census is particularly useful as there is a complete name index for the whole country; soldiers quartered in barracks in England and Wales should all be there (unless they were on leave on census day).

Searching the records pre-First World War

There is a great variety of records, as described in Simon Fowler's *Army Records for Family Historians*. The most used are:

1. Soldiers' documents (discharge papers) (reference WO 97) 1760-1913.
2. Pay Lists and Muster Rolls (reference WO 10 to WO 16) 1732-1898.
3. Description and Depot Books (reference WO26 and WO67) 1778-1908.

Try the soldiers' documents first.

1.   Soldiers' Documents (discharge papers), 1760-1913

For soldiers who were discharged at completion of their period of service, or discharged wounded, medically unfit or unstable for further service for some other reason - perhaps they had got involved in a pub brawl and been sent to gaol! Among these papers you will also find the discharge papers of men who bought themselves out of the Army after sometimes only a very short period of service. Except for the very early papers, these should give:

> place and date of birth
> appearance
> occupation (before joining up)
> army career
> wife/next of kin
> place of retirement (not all)
> date of death (not all).

The arrangement of these records varies according to date:

1760-1854

Strictly alphabetical modern name indexes are available in binders in the Research Enquiries Room and the Microfilm Reading Room. Better to use the on-line index via the computer terminal in the Microfilm Reading Room as there is cross-reference to aliases - many soldiers were known by more than one name!

Note the three-part reference (eg WO 97/203) and take the appropriate film from its cabinet in the Microfilm Reading Room.

1855-1872

Go to the binders for WO 97 in the lobby or Research Enquiries Room. The papers are arranged in alphabetical bundles *within regiments and corps*. Order the appropriate bundle on the computer. Collect it from the counter in the Document Reading Room and go through the papers to see if your soldier is there.

1873-1882

The papers are arranged in alphabetical bundles under the headings Cavalry, Artillery, Infantry and Corps. Consult the binders for WO 97 in the lobby or Research Enquiries Room and order the appropriate bundle on the computer. When it arrives, go through it and see if your soldier is there.

1883-1913

The papers for this period are arranged in alphabetical bundles (in two sequences,

Young Alfred Wilcox of Stratford, East London, joined the Royal Artillery briefly in 1889; previously he had worked for the Great Eastern Railway. His service record gives his parents' names and address, a resumé of his short military career and personal details of the lad himself — 'AW' (his initials) were tattooed on his left arm. (WO 97/4161)

Description of *Alfred Wilcox* on Enlistment.

Age physically equivalent to * __18__ years __11__ months.

Height __5__ feet __7½__ inches.

Weight† __133__ lbs.

Chest Measurement __34½__ inches.

Complexion __Sallow__

Eyes __Light hazel__

Hair __Brown__

Religious denomination __C. of E.__

‡ Distinctive Marks.

A. W. and dots on back of left forearm.

NOTE.—Civilian Medical Practitioners on making the primary examination of a recruit are to enter the above particulars in *pencil* only.
* To be determined according to the instructions given at para. 985 of the Medical Regulations, as amended by Clause 80, A. C., 1887, and to be filled in in all cases.
† A Civilian Medical Practitioner is not required to fill this in.
‡ Should the Medical Officer be of opinion that the recruit has served before, he will (unless the man acknowledges to any previous service) make a note to that effect in the column for distinctive marks.

CERTIFICATE OF PRIMARY MEDICAL EXAMINATION—(by a Civilian Medical Practitioner.)

No. *Alfred Wilcox*   MILITARY HISTORY SHEET.

1. Service at Home and Abroad (including former service of re-enlisted men, when allowed to reckon towards G. C. Pay or Pension).

COUNTRY	FROM	TO	YEARS	DAYS	N.B.—The Country only to be shown—it is not necessary to show separately the service in the different stations of same country. England, Scotland, and Ireland to be shown under the general term "Home." For mode of computing Foreign Service, see Sec. XIX., Queen's Regulations.
Home	5th March 1889	18 Apl 89		45	

		Initials of Officer making the Entry
2. Educated at ... {Royal Military Asylum / Royal Hibernian Military School}	No	*HWBe*
3. Name and Address of Next of Kin ... {Father Philip / Mother Elizabeth}	No 8 Francis Street, Stratford, Essex	
4. Campaigns ...	Nil	

STATEMENT of the SERVICES of No. RA *71313*   Name *Alfred Wilcox*

Corps in which served	Battn. or Depôt	Promotions, Reductions, Casualties, &c.	Army Rank	Dates	Service not allowed to reckon for fixing the rate of Pension		Service in Reserve not allowed to reckon towards G. C. Pay		Signature of Officer certifying correctness of Entries
					years	days	years	days	
		Service towards limited engagement reckons from		5 Mar 89					
Royal Artillery London Dist		Attested	Gunr	5 Mar 89					*W Murench major asupt RA record*
A Bde R.H.A.		Transferred	Gunr	16 Mar 89					
		Discharged on payment of £10.		18 Apl 89					*W Murench Major adupt RA Record*

1883-1900 and 1900-1913) by surname throughout the whole army. This makes your search much easier - unless your soldier has a common name; you may find twenty-five John Archers and not know which is yours unless you have his regiment or some other information to identify him.

Go to the binders labelled WO 97 in the lobby or Research Enquiries Room and order the bundle containing the appropriate part of the alphabet. Order it on the computer using the three-part reference, eg WO 97/3626. When it arrives search through and see if you can find your man.

2.   *Pay Lists and Muster Rolls, 1732-1898*

These are arranged by regiment

The records are quarterly returns listing all the men in each regiment or battalion. There is generally one volume for each year.

Consult the catalogues for WO 10 to WO 16 in the binders in the lobby or Research Enquiries Room. WO 10 relate to the Artillery, WO 11 Engineers, WO 12 General, WO 13 Militia and Volunteers, WO 14 Scutari Depot (Crimean War), WO 15 Foreign Legion and WO 16 all series after 1877. Select the appropriate lists and order them on the computer. The records will be produced in the Document Reading Room.

If you find your ancestor trace him back to his enlistment date when personal details are given. Then go forward to the time when he may appear in the list of 'men becoming non-effective' at the end of a return. This entry may also tell you when he joined the army and should give his date of death and the name of his widow or next of kin.

There are marriage rolls in the musters from 1868 which may give details of children as well as wives.

3.   *Description and Depot Description Books, 1778-1908*

The depot description books list men by depot, before they were assigned to a regiment. Description books are arranged by regiment, but do not survive for all regiments.

Only a relatively small percentage of soldiers appear in these records, but they are worth researching as the entries describe the men and give details of birth and career.

Consult the binders labelled WO 25 and WO 67. The description books for 1778-1878 are in WO 25/266-268. Order the records on the computer and they will be delivered to the Document Reading Room.

Other important sources

Pension records, Royal Chelsea Hospital, 1715-1913 (WO 116 and WO 117). Order records on the computer.

Medal Rolls, 1793-1912 (WO 100). These records give no genealogical details. They may be read on film in the Microfilm Reading Room.

There are many more useful sources as described in Simon Fowler's *Army Records for Family Historians.*

Records of soldiers ('other ranks') serving in the First World War

Consult the following before you start your research:

Army Service Records of the First World War, Simon Fowler et al. (PRO, 1996). You can read it in the Microfilm Reading Room or Research Enquiries Room, or buy it in the shop (£5.99).

The document pack *Battlefront: 1st July 1916 The first day of the Somme* (£9.99 in the PRO shop) shows how a soldier's service record can be linked to other PRO sources, such as trench maps and war diaries to give a picture of his role in the conflict.

About three million British subjects were mobilised in the First World War so there is a good chance that someone in your family served in the armed forces. The PRO has some service records (see below) and a complete set of indexed medal rolls. It is best to start with the latter.

Medal rolls

In seven cabinets in the centre of the Microfilm Reading Room you will find the microfiche name indexes to the medal rolls; gallantry medals are indexed separately from campaign medals.

Campaign medals

The vast majority of soldiers serving in the First World War were awarded campaign medals, so there is a good chance of finding your soldier here.

The medals were the 1914 Star (known as the 'Mons Star'), the 1914-15 Star, the British War Medal 1914-20, the Victory Medal 1914-19 and the Territorial Force War Medal 1914-1919. The Silver War Badge was awarded to men who had been discharged owing to sickness or wounds any time after 4 August 1914.

Three medals awarded to one man (either of the Stars and the British War and Victory medals) were nicknamed 'Pip, Squeak and Wilfred'. The British War and Victory medals on their own were known as 'Mutt and Jeff'.

Find yourself a fiche reader and remove the red card on it; this will be used to mark the place in the cabinet from where you have removed a fiche.

Now search through the fiche for the right part of the alphabet. If your soldier's name is common you might have a lot of searching to do. There are four fiches for the name Robert Davies, for instance. It will help immeasurably, unless the name you are after is uncommon, if you know the regiment.

Having found some likely entries on the fiche you will probably need the *Regimental List* (kept at the enquiry desk) to help you interpret the abbreviation for the name of the regiment. A leaflet is available which will help you to understand the rest of the information on the fiche - the name of the medal awarded and the theatre of war to which it relates.

Using the *Key to the Medal Roll Index* you can find the reference to the medal roll itself (class WO 329) and order the document on the computer. The roll entry often adds little to the index entry but it is worth a try.

If you find your ancestor on the fiche and discover he was awarded a gallantry medal, then you could search the indexes for the *London Gazette* which you will find in the cabinets in the Microfilm Reading Room. In some cases the citation which describes the act of gallantry was announced in this journal. The PRO's set of *Gazettes* is kept in a record class entitled ZJ 1. To read the *Gazette* entry, note the year, month and page in the index, consult the binder labelled ZJ 1 in the lobby or Research Enquiries Room and then order the relevant volume on the computer.

Service records

Only about forty per cent of the service records of men whose army career ended between 1914 and 1920 have survived; the rest having been destroyed in a bombing raid in 1940. The extant records, known as the 'Burnt Documents', are in the process of being transferred to the PRO from the Ministry of Defence (MOD). They are in a very fragile state, due to the effects of fire and water, but there is a project under way to microfilm them. As the films are completed they will be put into the record class WO 363.

A second collection of soldiers' documents was put together from duplicates held at the Ministry of Pensions. These are known as the 'Unburnt Documents' and make up record class WO 364. They are on film and can be read in the Microfilm Reading Room. There is about a one in ten chance of finding your soldier on these 4,000+ reels of microfilm. You are most likely to find him in this series if he was medically discharged.

The papers are arranged alphabetically. Consult the binder for WO 364 of which there are a number of copies in the Microfilm Reading Room. Note the item (piece) number which covers your soldier's name, eg:

> WO 364
>   956   Davies, Richard to Davies, Samuel

Then refer to the *Drawer Location List* which you should find on top of the microfilm cabinets. That will tell you that items (pieces) 915-962 are in 'dr. 920'. That includes no. 956, so help yourself to the film.

The papers may include a good deal of personal information, medical reports and family details as well as an account of your soldier's army career.

If his service records are not among those already in the PRO you could try applying to:

> Ministry of Defence CS(R)2b, Bourne Avenue, Hayes, Middlesex UB3 1RF. Tel: (for general information only) 0181 573 3831.

Write with as much information as you can. Ideally the MOD like a regiment name, service number and rough dates of service. If the name you are searching is uncommon they may be able to find something for you with only a name to go on. A fee of £20 is charged and you may have to wait several months for an answer.

Officers' records pre-First World War

You can construct an outline of an officer's career from the *Army List*, the red volumes on the shelves at the far end of the Microfilm Reading Room (also available in good reference libraries). They were published annually from 1754. The volumes on the open shelves start in 1798.

For the period 1839 to 1881 you can also try Hart's *Army List*. These volumes were published as an alternative to the official list and have many more details. The PRO set has manuscript notes appended which may give more information. They are on the shelves next to the *Army List* and there is also another set in the class WO 211.

Records of officers' services, 1764-1913, are in the classes WO 25 and WO 76. First look at the 21-drawer card index of officers in the Research Enquiries Room. This is incomplete (taken from WO 25 and WO 76), but very useful. If your officer is there the card will tell you when he was born, what his promotions were, what medals he won, who and when he married, when he retired and died.

To find the original records of his service, consult the binders for WO 25 and WO 76 and order the items you need on the computer.

For officers of the Artillery (to 1914) and Royal Engineers (to 1898) and Medical Officers (to 1960), there are published lists in the Research Enquiries Room.

Officers' records for the First World War

Personnel records for officers are due for transfer to the PRO in 1998 into the record class WO 374. In the meantime you can apply to the MOD at CS(RM)2, Bourne Avenue, Hayes, Middlesex UB3 1RF. For a £20 fee the MOD will do a search and supply you with details.

You can trace an officer's First World War career in the *Army Lists* in the Microfilm Reading Room (and reference libraries), through his medals (see pp 38-9) and there is often mention of officers in war diaries (see below).

War Diaries of the First World War

War diaries exist for most units. They are a daily record of events. Ordinary soldiers are rarely mentioned by name, but officers often are. Consult the binders labelled WO 95 and WO 154 and order the diary on the computer.

Army war dead

A list of men who died in the First World War was published in *Soldiers who died in the Great War* (HMSO, 1921). There is a microfilm copy in the Microfilm Reading Room. It is arranged by regiment.

You can apply to the Commonwealth War Graves Commission for information. They have records of all men who died or who were reported missing during the war. Their address is 2 Marlow Road, Maidenhead SL6 7DX.

The Militia, Yeomanry, Rifle Volunteers, Fencibles and Home Guard

From early times forces were raised in periods of emergency to protect the 'home front'. The records of theses forces are discussed in some detail in Garth Thomas's *Records of the Militia from 1757* (PRO Readers' Guide No. 3, 1993), which you can consult in the Research Enquiries Room. A new edition, revised by William Spencer, will be published in October 1997.

Records in the PRO include:

Militiamen's Attestation Papers, 1806-1915. Consult the binder labelled WO 96 in the lobby or Research Enquiries Room and order the records you require on the computer. The records, which are arranged alphabetically within regiment, give place and date of birth as well as career details. A list of militia regiments is given in Garth Thomas's book.

The careers of militia officers can be traced through the list of *Officers of the Several Regiments and Corps of the Militia* from 1794 and the *Army Lists* on the bookshelves in the Microfilm Reading Room.

Home Guard officers (October 1944) are listed in WO 199/3210-3217; consult the binder for WO 199 in the lobby or Research Enquiries Room and order the records you need on the computer.

Personal records and attestations of the Home Guard are at the Army Medal Office, Government Buildings, Worcester Road, Droitwich, Worcestershire WR9 8AU.

Personal records of the Territorial Army (founded 1908) are with the Ministry of Defence at CS(R)2b, Bourne Avenue, Hayes, Middlesex UB3 1RF.

BIRTHS, MARRIAGES AND DEATHS OF BRITONS ABROAD

The records of births, marriages and deaths registered in British embassies and consulates are to be found in a number of series in different places: PRO Kew, the Family Records Centre, the Guildhall Library, the Society of Genealogists and elsewhere. The records at PRO Kew are listed in the binders for RG32-RG36. There are name indexes on film (RG43) which can be consulted in the Microfilm Reading Room. Order the registers using a three-part reference such as RG 32/5, on the computer.

The indexes, but not the registers themselves, can also be read in the Family Records Centre in Myddelton Street. Consult *Never Been Here Before?* by Jane Cox (PRO Readers' Guide No. 17, revised ed. due for publication in August 1997).

To find out the whereabouts of other registers, consult Geoffrey Yeo's *The British Overseas* (Guildhall Library, 1988) in the Microfilm Reading Room.

British Empire and Commonwealth

Births, marriages and deaths registered in countries which were once part of the British Empire or Commonwealth are normally to be found among the archives of those countries. A guide to these records is *Abstract of Arrangements respecting Registration of Births, Marriages and Deaths etc* (General Register Office, 1952). A copy is kept in the Research Enquiries Room. Useful information is also found in *The British Overseas* (cited above).

The India Office Library (British Library Oriental and India Office Collections), 197 Blackfriars Road, London SE1 8NG, tel: 0171 412 7873, has about a thousand volumes containing births, marriages and deaths in India between 1698 and 1947.

Certification of death of Elizabeth Stanynought, aged 50, from Lambeth, headmistress of a school in Cahors, France, February 1836. From the register of births, marriages and deaths of British nationals in France, 1831-1871. (RG 35/9)

CEMETERY RECORDS

Before the mid-nineteenth century most burials took place in parish churches; there were some burial grounds for Nonconformists. Most registers kept by cemeteries are either in local record offices or still with the cemetery.

At PRO Kew you can see the records of the following:

The Bethnal Green Protestant Dissenters' Burying Ground or Gibraltar Row Burying Ground, 1793-1837 (reference RG 8/305-318)

Bunhill or Golden Lane Burial Ground, London, 1833-1853 (reference RG 8/35-38)

Victoria Park Cemetery, Hackney, 1852-1876 (reference RG 8/42-51).

Consult the binder labelled RG 8 in the lobby or Research Enquiries Room and order the records on the computer.

There are also lists of names (1601 to 1980, mainly nineteenth century) to be found among the records of a number of cleared burial grounds. Look through the list in the binder labelled RG 37 to see if there is a burial ground for your area and order the file on the computer.

See P F Wolfston's *Greater London Cemeteries and Crematoria* (Society of Genealogists, 1985) for the location of other London cemeteries.

Records of a few Nonconformist burial grounds are held at the Family Records Centre.

Many family history societies and/or local record offices have burial indexes for the areas with which they are concerned. The Society of Genealogists has Boyd's burial index for London and transcripts of many monumental inscriptions.

REGISTER of BURIALS. 31

Ann Buck — of the Parish of *St. M B Green* —
in the County of *Middlesex* aged *3 years 2 month*, was
buried in the Proteftant Diffenters Burying-Ground, in
on the *Twenty fifth* Day of *January* 1795
Regiftered the *Twenty fifth* Day of *January* 1795
By me *Ben Round* {Proteftant Diffenting Minifter.

197

25 26 by 61

John Counselman — of the Parish of *St. Peter le Poor* —
in the County of *Middlesex* aged *51 years* was
buried in the Proteftant Diffenters Burying-Ground, in
on the *Twenty fifth* Day of *January* 1795
Regiftered the *Twenty fifth* Day of *January* 1795
By me *Ben Round* {Proteftant Diffenting Minifter.

198

27 28 by 51

Catherine Jobber — of the Parish of *St. M B Y*
in the County of *Middlesex* aged *2 months* was
buried in the Proteftant Diffenters Burying-Ground, in
on the *Twenty fifth* Day of *January* 1795
Regiftered the *Twenty fifth* Day of *January* 1795
By me *Ben Round* {Proteftant Diffenting Minifter.

199

25 26 by 50

Catherine Jones of the Parish of *St. M Bishopgate*
in the County of *Middlesex* aged *27 years* was
buried in the Proteftant Diffenters Burying-Ground, in
on the *Twenty sixth* Day of *January* 1795
Regiftered the *Twenty sixth* Day of *February* 1795
By me *Ben Round* {Proteftant Diffenting Minifter.

200

13 by 3

Register of the Gibraltar Row Burial Ground, Mile End, East London, 1795.
(RG 8/305)

CHANGE OF NAME RECORDS

If your ancestor changed his name (many Jewish immigrants did, for example) you *may* be able to trace the records of this at PRO Kew, but only if the change of name was centrally registered - the majority were not.

Most of the indexes you need to use are kept in the Map and Large Document Room on the second floor and the records of change of name are produced there.

1760-1901: consult *An Index to Changes of Name, 1760-1901*, ed. W P W Phillimore and E A Fry (London, 1905) on the bookshelves.

Late nineteenth century to 1992: go through the volumes of indexes to the Close Rolls and Enrolment Books on the bookshelves. Then order the relevant documents on the computer using the instructions pasted into the beginning of the volumes. Class references are C 54 (pre-1903) and J 18 (post-1903).

From 1914 deed polls were announced in the *London Gazette*. The *London Gazette Index of Changes of Name 1934 to 1964* and other indexes (ask at the enquiry desk) will tell you which editions of the *Gazette* to look at. The *Gazette* is in record class ZJ 1; consult the binder thus labelled in the lobby or Research Enquiries Room (first floor) and order the appropriate volume on the computer.

For name changes since 1992 you can get information from The Deed Poll Department, The Royal Courts of Justice, London WC2A 1LL. Tel: 0171 936 6000 x 6528.

COASTGUARD SERVICE RECORDS

PRO Kew has service records for the Coastguard for the whole of the British Isles, from 1822 to 1947. The main series of records is in class ADM 175. Consult the binder thus labelled in the lobby or Research Enquiries Room and order the relevant items on the computer, using a three-part reference such as ADM 175/90. Some of the records are on film and you will be able to help yourself in the Microfilm Reading Room; some are large and will be produced in the Map and Large Document Room; some are produced in the main Document Reading Room.

You will find an information leaflet on coastguards in the pigeon holes in the lobby.

For a small fee you can save yourself a good deal of time by writing to Mrs Eileen Stage who has a coastguard index. Her address is 150 Fulwell Park Avenue, Twickenham, Middlesex TW2 5BH.

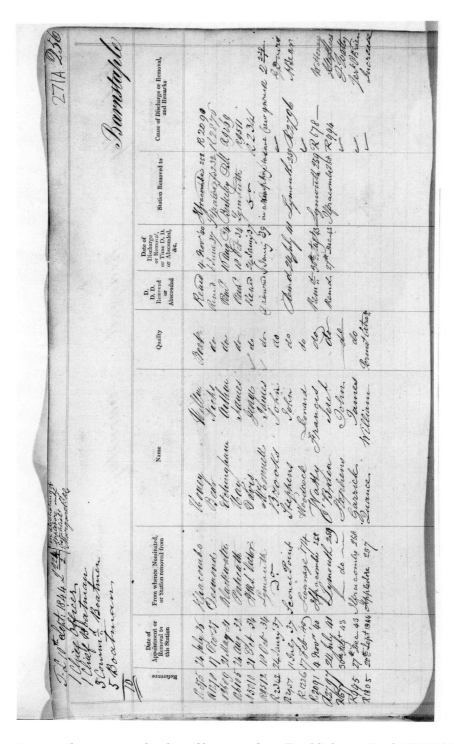

Barnstaple coastguards: list of boatmen from Establishment Book 1833-1844. (ADM 175/90 f.271A)

CRIME, CONVICTS AND TRANSPORTATION

PRO Kew has records of trials going back to the Middle Ages. Records before 1733 are largely in Latin.

For records of crime and criminals from the eighteenth century you would do well to consult David Hawkings' *Criminal Ancestors* (Stroud, 1992), which describes and lists an enormous range of records both in the PRO and elsewhere. You can read it in the Research Enquiries Room or buy the 1996 paperback edition in the shop. You may also find useful Michelle Cale's *Law and Society* (PRO Readers' Guide No. 14, 1996).

Petty crime was dealt with at a local level by the Lord of the Manor's Court or Justices of the Peace at Quarter Sessions. The records of their proceedings are usually in local record offices.

More serious offences were dealt with by the Justices of Assize who travelled around the country. You can research the records of the Assizes and the Central Criminal Court at PRO Kew.

Finding the records of a trial at the Assizes

Appendix 4 of *Criminal Ancestors* lists surviving assize records in detail and appendix 7 lists the records county by county. A PRO information leaflet on assize records (you can get this from the pigeon holes in the first floor lobby) provides similar information, but not in such detail. Most assize records are in the PRO, but Bristol records before 1832 are held in the Bristol record office.

Assize records are classified by 'circuit', the routes taken by the judges. If you know the county your ancestor came from but not where he was tried, consult appendix 7 of *Criminal Ancestors* first.

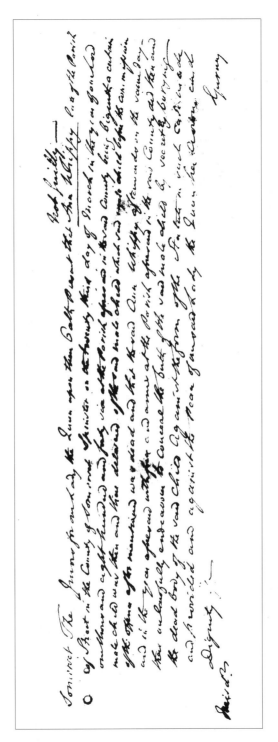

Ann Whippy of Street, Somerset, found not guilty of concealing the birth and death of her stillborn son. Indictment, March 1746. (ASSI 25/33/11)

Let us suppose your ancestor murdered his brother in Kings Lynn in 1670. By referring to David Hawkings or the PRO leaflet you will learn that the crime would have been dealt with by the Justices on the Norfolk Circuit. The main series of records is called 'indictments'; you will learn from the leaflet/David Hawkings that Norfolk Circuit indictments *do* survive from the seventeenth century (you are lucky) and they are classified as ASSI 16.

Find the binder labelled ASS1 16 in the lobby or Research Enquiries Room and note the reference for the bundle of indictments for 1670 (ASSI 16/19) and order it on the computer.

The indictment (and crown book, if one survives) will give you the barest outline details of the case, and a note of the outcome of the trial. There are rarely any personal details, and it is a good idea to look for a report of the crime in the local press. You will have to go to a local studies library or the British Library Newspaper Library, at Colindale Avenue, London NW9 5HE for that; consult Jeremy Gibson's *Local Newspapers, 1750-1920* (Federation of Family History Societies, 1987), to see what papers survive and where they may be read. *Local Newspapers* is available in the Research Enquiries Room and for sale in the shop.

Finding a trial at the Old Bailey in London

The equivalent to Assizes for the City of London and Middlesex was sessions held before the Lord Mayor at the Old Bailey.

Pre-1834 Old Bailey records are in the Corporation of London Record Office, Guildhall, London EC2P 2EJ (London trials) and the London Metropolitan Archives (former Greater London Record Office), 40 Northampton Road, London EC1R 0HB (Middlesex trials). An incomplete set of full and informative printed proceedings is at PRO Kew, reference PCOM 1, 1801-1904. A complete set is kept at the Guildhall Library, Aldermanbury, London EC2P 2EJ.

After 1834 the records of the Central Criminal Court, as it was now called, are in the PRO, the main series being indictments (CRIM 4; use CRIM 5 as an index). It is probably best to start with the indexed transcripts of these trials at the Guildhall Library, *Old Bailey Sessions' Papers*.

To research the CRIM records, find the binders labelled CRIM 4 and CRIM 5 and order the records you want on the computer.

Transportation

Criminal ancestors who were deported to American (1616-1775) or Australian (1787-1868) penal colonies are not difficult to trace. There is an abundance of documentation. David Hawkings' book, cited above, takes you through the maze of records available both in the PRO and elsewhere with great clarity.

As a first step look up your ancestor in one of the published lists of deportees given below. You will find them on the shelves in the Research Enquiries Room or the Library; MORIS will tell you where they are (see pp 20-21):

P W Coldham, *Complete Book of Emigrants in Bondage, 1614-1775* (Baltimore, 1987). This book draws on a variety of sources; ask a member of staff to explain to you what these are and how you can consult the original records, such as Port Books.

Census of New South Wales, 1828, ed M R Sainty and K A Johnson (Baltimore, 1987). This book contains all the information in the original census.

There is, in private hands, an index of many thousands of names of people who left the UK for America, Canada and the West Indies, 1600-1850. Write to Mr F Leeson, 108 Sea Lane, Ferring, Sussex BN12 5HB.

After the NSW census the most useful record classes for transportees to Australia are:

Criminal registers, one series for London and Middlesex, and one for the rest of the country (from 1791, reference HO 26 and HO 27). These list

122. Names of Offenders	Degree of Instruction	Ages	At what Sessions Tried or Discharged without Trial	Offence of which those Tried were Convicted or Acquitted—and of which those Recharged without Trial were charged on Indictment or Commitment
Layton, Henry	R	10	County Sessions Clerkenwell — 30th December	Larceny
Low, William	Imp	37	Do	Assault
Lechmere, Thomas Luther	Imp	72	Do	Misdmr. Keeping a furious dog
Lovelock, James	Imp	25	Do	Larceny
Lyon, Ezekiel	Imp	27	Central Criminal Court 6th January	Do
Lewis, John	Well	40	Do	Do
Locke, Mary	R	19	Do	Larceny from the Person
Levey, Lewis	Imp	20	Do	Larceny
Long, James	Imp	18	Do	Larceny by Servant
Lemage, Frances	Well	24	Do	Larceny from the Person
Lambert, Ann	Imp	21	Central Criminal Court 3rd February	Larceny
Lovegrove, John	R	19	Do	Larceny from the Person
Linan, Joseph	Imp	12	Do	Larceny
Lloyd, John	R	11	Do	Do
Lippia, Mary Ann (or Ann Book)	R	45	Do	Uttering a forged Warrant. (Bef.)
Lye, Francis	Well	31	Do	Stealing a fixture
Long, Elizabeth	Imp	22	Do	Larceny
Lown, William	Well	58	Do	Assault with an Unnatural Intent
Lewis, Edward	Imp	47	Do	Assault
Lee, George	R	11	Do	Larceny

Criminal Register, Middlesex 1840. *(HO 26/46 ff.120-121) at the Assizes and Sessions held within the County during the Year 1840.*

	SENTENCES			Acquittals	Execution or Commutation of Capital Sentences
Death	Transportation	Imprisonment	Whipping, Fine, &c.		
			8 Days and Whipped		
			Fined 1/		
				Not Guilty	
				No Bill	
	7 Years				
	7 Years				
		6 Months			
		3 Months			
				Not Guilty	
				No Bill	
				Not Guilty	
	10 Years				
	7 Years				
	7 Years				
		2 Years			
		3 Months			
		3 Months			
		1 Year			
		1 Year			
		4 Days			

convicts alphabetically and also give the date and place of their trial.

Convict transportation registers (1787-1871, reference HO 11, 21 volumes). They list convict ships and the names of the unfortunate souls carried in each, giving the date and place of conviction. The arrangement is by port of departure and there is a card index in the Research Enquiries Room.

To read these records consult the binders containing the lists of HO 11, HO 26 or HO 27 in the lobby or Research Enquiries Room and order the items you want on the computer.

Now you have found out where your ancestor was tried, you will probably want to look at the records of his/her trial. If he/she was tried at the Quarter Sessions you will have to go to the appropriate local record office. If he/she was tried at the Assizes you will be able to find the records on the second floor at PRO Kew, as described above.

CUSTOMS AND EXCISE OFFICERS

There are staff lists and superannuation registers for customs officers, 1671-1922 (closed for seventy-five years), some of which may give personal details. The series of records (reference CUST 39) is, however, very incomplete. The pay lists (CUST 18 and CUST 19, 1675-1829) give name and post only (sometimes only the post!).

Excise officers are better documented. Their entry papers (CUST 116, 1820-1870) include letters of recommendation with age, place of birth, marital status and a 'character'. There is a card index in the Research Enquiries Room.

To order these records, find the binders labelled CUST in the lobby or Research Enquiries Room and order the relevant items on the computer.

May it please your Honors.

These are to certify, that Edwin Abbott, born at Deal, in the parish of Deal, in the county of Kent, in Canterbury collection, aged twenty years, is instructed, pursuant to your Honors' order, bearing date, the thirtieth day of July, 1858, and is qualified for surveying, maltsters, distillers, paper makers, rectifiers, brewers, tobacco manufacturers, spirit retailers, and tobacco dealers.

He can cast gauges, both by pen and rule; has surveyed for six weeks in Stepney 3rd Division, and duly entered his surveys in books prepared by him for that purpose, from which he has made true vouchers and abstracts.

He is provided with proper instruments and instruction, and well qualified in every respect for the employment of a Surveying officer of Inland Revenue.

   Charles Snelgrove Supervisor.
   John Henderson Officer.

Dated at 8, Queens Row, Cambridge road; the eighteenth day of September, 1858.

I have examined the above mentioned Edwin Abbott, and find him fully qualified, as above stated.

   Thomas Dean   Collector.

Dated, at the Inland Revenue Office, Tower Hill, the eighteenth day of September, 1858.

Letter of recommendation for Excise Officer: Edwin Abbott, 1858. (CUST 116/42)

DEATH DUTY RECORDS

***These records, which complement and supplement wills, can be read either at
PRO Kew or at the Family Records Centre, depending on the year you require:***

1796-1857 at the Family Records Centre.

1858-1903 at PRO Kew (give five days' notice when ordering these records
as they are stored off-site).

Indexes 1796-1903 at *both* the Family Records Centre and PRO Kew.

The Death Duty records are one of the most important genealogical sources in
the PRO. The 8,000 registers and their indexes document the levying of a series
of different duties and provide;

- a countrywide probate index (not comprehensive) for the period 1796-1858

- information about many thousands of families, their wealth, possessions
  and landed property which often supplements what is to be found in wills
  and grants of administration.

*Death Duty records are one of the most useful genealogical sources
in the PRO, but you may need help to interpret them.*

You may find it useful to consult *Prerogative Court of Canterbury Wills and
Other Probate Records*, Miriam Scott (PRO Readers' Guide No. 15, 1997).

Using the Death Duty indexes (reference IR 27, at PRO Kew and the Family Records Centre) as a countrywide probate index

Before 1858 there were over three hundred probate courts and the wills and administrations dealt with therein are now deposited in different record offices all over the country; there are no central indexes to them. (Grants of administration, normally abbreviated to 'admons', might be made if no will had been made).

One way of finding an ancestor's will/administration is by checking through the microfilm of the Death Duty indexes. These indexes are not a comprehensive guide to all wills/administrations, but they cover a good many. Duty was not payable on very small estates.

1796-1815

Only a small percentage of estates were dutiable during this period, so the indexes are slim and the chances of finding a particular individual are not as high as they become later. The Duty, at this stage, was limited to legacies and residues left to people who were *not* close relatives. Thus wills which benefited only wives, children, parents and grandparents will not appear at all.

1815-1858

For this period there is far wider coverage. In 1854 there was said to be a Death Duty entry for one out of every sixteen people who died in the country.

Finding your way round the indexes (IR 27)

The indexes are on film and can be read at Kew and the Family Records Centre.

Consult the binder for IR 27 in the Microfilm Reading Room. You will see that the 605 volumes are in various series according to whether the will/admon was from the Prerogative Court of Canterbury (PCC) or a country court.

For the period 1796-1811 there are surname indexes on the bookshelves for certain county courts. There is a card index for some and a typescript index for others. They will tell you all you need to know - you don't have to bother with the film.

Note the reference for the film you need (eg IR 27/339) and take it from the cabinet. Wind the film on until you find your ancestor's name. Note the court where the probate/admon was granted (fourth column) and the register number (fifth column) and the folio number (sixth column).

Having noted the name of the court where the grant was made, you will be able to find out where to go to read the will/admon. The courts are referred to by abbreviation: PY for Prerogative Court of York, Archd. for archdeaconry court, Const. for bishop's consistory court etc. Use Jeremy Gibson's *Probate Jurisdictions, Where to Look for Wills* (FFHS, 4th edn 1994 - borrow from enquiry desk or buy in shop) to find out what courts there are and which record office now has the wills/admons. If the fourth column of the index says 'PC', then the will/admon is in the PRO and you can read it at Kew *or* in the Family Records Centre.

The register number and folio number are your way into the Death Duty registers themselves.

Testator	Residence	Executors	Court	Register	Folio
Shore, John Wood	Sheffield	George Hemsoll & ors	PY	2	502
Shute, William	Kingston Magna	Stephen Read & ors	Dorset	2	603
Shoemack, James	Teddington	H C Shoemack & Brompton	PC	3	728

Sample entries in Death Duty Index (IR/27/323; register for wills 1857 'S' to 'Z'). John Shore's will is in the Borthwick Institute of Historical Research (Prerogative Court of York); William Shute's will is in the Dorset County Record Office; and James Shoemack's will is in the PRO.

Using the Death Duty registers to supplement information in wills/ admons

The entries in the registers may add considerably to what you have found out in a will or grant of administration. Entries relating to intestate estates (admons) may be especially useful, as beneficiaries may be listed with addresses and other information. Bequeathed items may be specifically valued and the names and addresses of family members may be given, perhaps spanning several generations as the revenue officers chase up individuals. After 1853 there is information about the descent of landed property.

Remember that entries cover wills proved in all courts including those proved after 1858 now in the Principal Registry of the Family Division at Somerset House (see p 7). It is these later registers which you can read at Kew. The registers for 1796-1858 can be read at the Family Records Centre.

Finding an entry in a Death Duty register (IR 26)

Use the IR 27 indexes as described above to get the register and folio number for your individual. Now take the binder for IR 26 and key this up - remember the registers are in different series. You will need a three-part reference such as IR 26/98. This is a register number; when it comes, find the folio number which you have got from the index.

You will have to make two trips to the PRO to find a Death Duty entry for 1858-1904. The registers are not stored in the building and you should allow five days' notice for them to be delivered to PRO Kew. Get the reference on your first trip, order the document and come back five days later to read it. Alternatively, you can get the reference from the Family Records Centre and telephone your order to Kew.

Understanding the entries

The registers are complicated and there is a series of abbreviations. You will need to consult Jane Cox, *Never Been Here Before? a guide to the Family Records Centre* (PRO, 1997). The abbreviations are also listed in the information leaflet on Death Duties which you will find in the pigeon holes in the first floor lobby.

DIVORCE RECORDS

1941 to date

For this period divorce records are in the Principal Registry of the Family Division at Somerset House, Strand, London WC2R 1LP. For a fee a search will be done for you. Tel: 0171 936 6931 for information. The PRO indexes (J 78) go up to 1958.

1858-1940

For this period divorce files are in the PRO in J 77, with indexes in J 78. Find the binder labelled J 78 in the lobby or Research Enquiries Room and order the relevant index on the computer. Having found your divorce in the index, order the file on the computer using a three-part reference such as J 77/100.

The files may contain petitions for divorce and judicial separation, declarations of legitimacy, a copy of the petition and grounds for divorce.

Some files are subject to an extended closure period of seventy-five years.

Pre-1858

Until 1677 divorce was illegal (unless you were Henry VIII). After 1677 it became legal, but was rare, and achieved only by Act of Parliament. The original records are in the House of Lords Record Office, Palace of Westminster, London SW1 OPW. Tel: 0171 219 5316.

Legal separations might be granted by the church courts, and the records of these proceedings are deposited in local (diocesan) record offices. The London Consistory Court did a good deal of matrimonial business; the records are in the London Metropolitan Archives, 40 Northampton Road, London EC1R OAB.

IN THE HIGH COURT OF JUSTICE

PROBATE DIVORCE AND ADMIRALTY DIVISION

(DIVORCE)

TO THE RIGHT HONOURABLE THE PRESIDENT

THE second day of April 1937.

THE HUMBLE PETITION OF FLORENCE MARY BROACHES-CARTER.

S H E W E T H :-

1.   THAT on the 31st day of October, 1925, your ----
Petitioner, then Florence Mary Part, Spinster, was --
lawfully married to Bernard Purvis Broaches-Carter ---
(hereinafter called "the Respondent") at the Cathedral
and Parish Church of Manchester in the County of
Lancaster.

2.   THAT after the said marriage your Petitioner and
the Respondent lived and cohabited at divers places and
finally at 29 Mayfield Road, Whalley Range, Manchester
aforesaid and there is no issue of the marriage.

3.   THAT your Petitioner is now living at "Ormesby",
133, The Avenue, Leigh, in the County of Lancaster that
the Respondent who is an Electrical Engineer is now ---
living at 13 Coleherne Road, Earls Court, London,S.W.10
and that both the Petitioner and the Respondent are ---
domiciled in England.

4.   THAT there have been no previous proceedings in this
Honourable Court with reference to your Petitioner's
said marriage either by or on behalf of your Petitioner
or the Respondent.

5.   THAT the Respondent has frequently committed ----
adultery with Hermia Dean.

6.   THAT on the 2nd, 3rd and 4th days of March, 1937
at the Cumberland Hotel, Marble Arch, London, W.1. the
Respondent lived and cohabited and committed adultery
with Hermia Dean.

YOUR PETITIONER therefore prays that your Lordship
will decree:-

(1) That the said Marriage be dissolved.

(2) That your Petitioner may have such further and
other relief as may be just.

Divorce petition of Florence Broaches-Carter; her husband of twelve years has been committing adultery at the Cumberland Hotel with one Hermia Dean, April 1937. (J 77/3746)

DOCKYARD WORKERS' RECORDS

Take the information leaflet *Dockyard Employees* from the pigeon holes in the first floor lobby. This lists the surviving records from 1660 of British naval dockyards all over the world, which include yard musters and lists, giving information on the many different tradesmen employed by the yards, their entry and discharge, pay, pension arrangements and other details.

References to the main sources for service records (some of which give personal details) are to be found in the binders labelled ADM 32, ADM 36, ADM 42 and ADM 106. Find the item you want and order it on the computer.

EMIGRANTS

From 1890

If you know (or can guess) the port your ancestor left from in the UK and roughly when he/she left (between 1890 and 1960), then you should search the passenger lists (reference BT 27). Entries give name, age, occupation and some sort of address. Only people leaving the UK for destinations outside Europe and the Mediterranean are included.

The registers of ships' passenger lists (reference BT 32) list the ships leaving each port and may be a help to you in finding the right BT 26 register. The BT 32 registers are on the shelves in the Research Enquiries Room. The passenger lists themselves have to be ordered on the computer; most of them are very large volumes and will be delivered to the Map and Large Document Room. You may need to go through a number of registers, so remember to order three registers at a time and then three more as soon as the original three have arrived - and so on.

Emigrants to North America pre-1890

For criminal transportees and deportees to 1775 see under 'Crime, Convicts and Transportation' pp 50-56).

There is **no regular documentation of people leaving the country**, and if you are in search of an ancestor who you think came from the UK the best place to start may well be the IGI (see p 8) for the pre-1837 period. If he/she was in the UK in 1881, then by far the best place to start the search is the name index to the 1881 census which you can see in the Family Records Centre and at LDS (Mormon) Family History Centres. The census tells you where people came from, so you should be able to identify your ancestor.

There is a range of scattered sources for people leaving the country, the most obvious being Licences to Pass Beyond the Seas (reference E 157). These were an early form of passport; some emigrants were issued with them, others not. A great deal of research has been done on emigration to America and many of the sources, including the Licences, have been used in the compilation of numbers of name indexes. Start with these.

On the shelves at PRO Kew (MORIS will tell you where, see p 20) you will find:

New World Immigrants, ed M Tepper (Baltimore, 1980)

Passenger and Immigration Lists, ed P W Filby and M K Meyer (Michigan, 1981-5), contains 500,000 names, USA and Canada

A List of Immigrants from England to America, 1718-1759, J and M Kaminkov (Baltimore, 1964)

Original Lists of Persons emigrating to America, 1600-1800, J C Hotten (London, 1874).

Two vast compilations are held in private hands; information will be supplied for a small fee:

Mr F Leeson of 108 Sea Lane, Ferring, Sussex BN12 5HB has a name index to about one hundred published and unpublished sources for emigrants to Canada, America and the West Indies, 1660-1850.

Mr N Currer-Briggs of 3 High Street, Sutton in the Isles, Cambs CB6 2RB has an index of about fifty thousand names of emigrants to the southern colonies of America, compiled from sources in England and Virginia, 1560-1690.

People who suffered losses because of their loyalty to Britain during the American War of Independence could claim compensation. Lists of pensioners and supporting papers are to be found among the Treasury records. Find the binders labelled TS 50 and TS 79 and order the relevant records on the computer.

More sources are suggested in the PRO information leaflet, *Emigrants, Documents in the Public Record Office.*

For emigrants to the West Indies consult Guy Grannum's *Tracing your West Indian Ancestry* (PRO Readers' Guide No. 11, 1995). You can read it in the Research Enquiries Room or buy it in the shop for £8.95.

Emigrants to Australia pre-1890

For transportees to the penal colony before 1868 see pp 53-56.

Those who went of their own accord to Australia are more difficult to track down than transportees and, as mentioned above, it may be best to start your search for an English ancestor by looking for him/her in the IGI in the Microfilm Reading Room (see p 8) (for the pre-1837 period) or the index to the 1881 census at the Family Records Centre and at LDS (Mormon) Family History Centres. For both these indexes it will speed things up if you know roughly where he/she might have come from, as the arrangement is by county.

If your ancestor had left the UK by 1828 you can look him up in the published New South Wales census (cited on p 53) in the Research Enquiries Room.

IMMIGRANTS

There is ***no regular documentation of foreigners entering the country***, so you cannot be sure that you will find any records of your ancestor's arrival here. It may be best to start with some of the tried and true (and indexed) sources which lead you to him *in situ* in this country.

If he was a nineteenth-century immigrant, such as a Jew arriving from Eastern Europe in the 1880s, or an Irishman fleeing the Famine, you are probably best advised to start by looking for him in the census. There is a partial name index to the 1851 census and a complete one for 1881, which you can see at the Family Records Centre. The arrangement is by county.

Earlier (religious) refugees like Huguenots are probably best sought in the records of the chapels they joined, which are described on p 92 in the section on Nonconformist records. The Huguenot Society has published numerous lists of immigrants. Ask MORIS (the PRO's computerized guide to reference works) what lists are available to be read in the Research Enquiries Room.

Your immigrant ancestor may have thought it wise to change his name; there may be a record of this in PRO Kew (see p 47). If he settled down and made a success of his life he may have left a will. See p 113.

Naturalization and denization records, 1801-1935

Some foreigners took out naturalizations or denizations, though far from all. Denization gave some of the privileges of naturalization; a denizen could purchase and devise land but not inherit it. Check the binder labelled HO 1 in the first floor lobby or Research Enquiries Room. This is an alphabetical list of names. Find your man and order the record itself on the computer.

Passenger Lists from 1890

Consult the ships' inward passenger lists (reference BT 26). Only ships coming from outside Europe are included and there are *no name indexes*. It helps if you know the date of arrival and port of entry - if not, you may be in for an extremely long search.

Abraham Isaac Marks of the Borough of " "
Sunderland in the County of Durham General Merchant
maketh oath and saith that he is a native of " " "
Wongrowitz in the province of Posen in the Kingdom
of Prussia that he is of the age of thirty years. That
he is a General Merchant and carries on business at
the said Borough of Sunderland. That he has resided
in Great Britain during the last fifteen " " years
and that he has been married to an English lady for
the last ten " " years by whom he has a family
And that he intends to make Great Britain the place
of his future residence, that he is well affected to Her
Majesty's power and Government

Sworn at the Borough of Sunderland
in the County of Durham the " "
sixteenth " day of February one
thousand eight hundred and fifty

A I Marks

Before Me

A Master Extraordinary
in Chancery

Naturalisation oath of Abraham Isaac Marks, immigrant from Prussia, 1850.
(HO 1/32/1081)

IMMIGRATION.

N.B.—By sec. 100 of the Passengers Act, 1855, the Master of every Ship bringing Passengers *into* the United Kingdom, is required, under a penalty not exceeding £50, to deliver to the Emigration Officer, or in his absence to the Chief Officer of Customs at the Port of Arrival, a correct List signed by such Master, and specifying the names, ages, and callings of all the Passengers embarked, and also the Port or Ports at which they respectively may have embarked, and showing which, if any, of them may have died, with the supposed cause of death, or been born on the voyage.

FORM OF PASSENGER LIST.

Ship's Name.	Official No.	Tons per Register.	Master's Name.	Aggregate number of superficial feet in the several compartments set apart for Passengers, other than Cabin Passengers.	Total number of Statute Adults, exclusive of Master, Crew, and Cabin Passenger, which the Ship can legally carry.	Voyage.
Spartan		2029	Am McLean Wait			From Cape Town To Southampton

NAMES AND DESCRIPTIONS OF PASSENGERS.

(The Names, &c., of Cabin Passengers to be entered on page 3.)

Ports of Embarkation.	Names of Passengers.	Age of each Adult of Twelve years & upwards. Married M.	Married F.	Single M.	Single F.	Children between 1 & 12 Years. M.	Children between 1 & 12 Years. F.	Infants. M.	Infants. F.	Profession, Occupation, or Calling of Passengers.	English.	Scotch.	Irish.	Foreigners.	Ports at which Passengers have been landed.
	First Class Passengers Cabin														
Natal	Major Warton	44								Retired army officer	1				Southampton
	Mr Christian				31					Gentleman	1				
	Mr Jardine	35								Merchant			1		
	Mrs "		34										1		
	Miss "					1							1		
	Mr H Jardine	71								Retired Merchant			1		
	Mr Little	49								Merchant	1				
	Mrs "		44								1				
	Master "					1					1				
	Master "					1					1				
	Master "					1					1				
	Master "					1					1				
	Miss "						1				1				
	Miss "						1				1				
	Mrs Tilney		57							Lady		1			
	Mrs G. A. Tilney				24					Lady		1			
	Miss Tilney						1				1				
	Nurse (2nd)				27						1				
	Mr Buckworth	21								Student	1				

Part of list of passengers arriving from Natal at Southampton, May 1890.   (BT 26/7)

LEGAL RECORDS: CIVIL ACTIONS

For criminal records see pp 50-56.

The PRO holds the surviving records of all the central law courts from medieval times, covering disputes about land, debts, inheritance, trusts, fraud, marriage settlements, wills, etc.

If you know that your family was involved in a lawsuit it should be possible to find the proceedings, especially if you know which court they went to and when it was.

The courts of Common Law were: King's Bench (KB), Common Pleas (CP), the Exchequer of Pleas (E), the Common Law side of Chancery (C) and the Assizes (ASSI). Proceedings at Common Law relied largely on *viva voce* cross examination in court. The records are not very informative and they are in Latin until 1733.

There were also courts of equity: Chancery, (C) the Court of Requests (REQ), Star Chamber (STAC), the equity side of the Exchequer (E) etc. For these courts there are written proceedings (in English) which are a goldmine for the family historian and, what is more, our ancestors sued one another at the drop of a hat, so the chances of finding litigation in your family are relatively good.

There were special courts for the palatinates of Chester, Durham, Lancaster and Wales. The records of all these (except Wales) are in the PRO. The Welsh records are in the National Library of Wales, Penglais, Aberystwyth SY23 3BU.

There was a separate legal system, called 'Civil Law' which was based on Roman Law and ecclesiastical law; the 'Civilians', as they were called, sorted out disputes over 'wills, wrecks and wives' (probate, shipboard disputes and piracy and matrimonial affairs) in courts in Doctors' Commons, in London. These were the High Court of Admiralty, the Prerogative Court of Canterbury and various other church courts. The records of the High Court of Admiralty (HCA) and the Prerogative Court of Canterbury (PCC) are in the PRO, along with the records of the appeal court for Civil matters, the High Court of Delegates (DEL).

In the mid-nineteenth century all these courts (common law and equity, civil and criminal) were brought together (except the Assizes and the church courts) into a single Supreme Court of Judicature. The records of this court are classified as 'J' in the PRO. The central law courts all sat in Westminster Hall until the end of the nineteenth century.

Research into legal records is a complicated matter and you may need help from PRO staff. Apply to the desk in the Research Enquiries Room or the Map and Large Document Room, as many legal records are large and are seen there. Some elements of civil law records are explained in *Law and Society, An Introduction to Sources for Criminal and Legal History from 1800*, Michelle Cale (PRO Readers' Guide No. 14, 1996).

Assizes

The Justices of Assize, who travelled round the country, dealt with both crime and civil matters. See pp 50-52 for a description of Assize records.

To find a case in the Assizes, first find out which circuit (route travelled by the judges) covered the part of the country where your family lived. You can do this by looking at the leaflet on Assize records in the pigeon holes in the lobby. The records for most of the country bear the reference ASSI; the records of the palatinates of Durham, Lancaster and Chester are designated as DURH, PL and CHES respectively. Bristol Assize records are held in the Bristol Record Office.

Find the binder with the right class label (ASSI, etc) in the lobby or Research Enquiries Room and look though the list for records described as *posteas* and *minute books*. These are the records which relate to civil litigation (known as *nisi prius*). Order the item you want on the computer.

You won't get much information about the case - probably just a brief note of its nature, the parties involved and the outcome, amount of damages etc. There may be a newspaper report. Use Jeremy Gibson's *Local Newspapers* (cited on p 52) to see whether any newspapers survive for your area.

Chancery suits

For Chancery searches in the PRO go to the Map and Large Document Room.

Our ancestors sued one another at the drop of a hat

The busiest court for litigation and the one where you are most likely to find your family 'at war' was the Court of Chancery. These legal records are in English.

Finding your ancestors in Chancery

The court was in operation from the fourteenth century until 1875, when it became the Chancery Division of the Supreme Court. The records are classified as 'C' before 1875 and as 'J' thereafter. It dealt with disputed wills, trusts, marriage settlements, frauds, land disputes etc.

1600-1800 *The Bernau Index at the Society of Genealogists*

To find a specific case, or for a speculative search to see if your family engaged in litigation during this period, the best place to start is the Society of Genealogists (see page 8). The PRO has no cumulative name index and the nearest thing is the Bernau index to plaintiffs, defendants and witnesses (deponents). Note all the parts of the reference which is given and return to PRO Kew. A useful guide is Hilary Sharp's *How to Use the Bernau Index* (SOG, 1996) which explains its coverage and the abbreviations used.

Ask the staff at the enquiry desk in the Map and Large Document Room to check your reference and then key it into the computer.

When your record is delivered you may find that it is a very large sheet. This is a 'bill' or 'answer' and is a summary of the argument produced by the plaintiff or defendant ('proceedings', see p 76). To read it you will need a long ruler (one is kept at the enquiry desk) to stop your eye slipping down to the line beneath.

......a very large sheet indeed

If it is not a 'bill' or 'answer' (or a 'rejoinder' or 'replication') it may be a 'deposition' - the evidence about a case given by a witness.

Late 17th century   *The Coldham indexes to wills in Chancery*

A high percentage of Chancery business was concerned with wills and intestate estates. P W Coldham's *Indexes to disputed estates in Chancery* (indexes to proceedings in classes C 6, C 7, C 8 & C 10) is a good way of locating these cases as the Coldham indexes are arranged by the name of the dead man, whereas the normal Chancery indexes (not Bernau) are arranged by plaintiff only. MORIS will tell you where they are.

14th century to 1942   *The indexes to the Decree and Order Books*

These indexes are a series of volumes kept on the open shelves in the Map and Large Document Room. The Decree and Order Books themselves (C 33) record the court's decisions and provide the 'bones' of the case. Proceedings and evidences etc are then used to complete the story.

The indexes are annual volumes, one for each half of the alphabet ('A' & 'B' books), arranged by the initial letter of the plaintiff's name. You can browse through them at your leisure. If you find an entry, carry on looking - Chancery cases could drag on for years and years. When you find your case note the term, the year and the number. The law terms were Hilary (starting January), Easter, Trinity (May/June) and Michaelmas (autumn). *Remember that before 1752 the year started on March 25th so what appears to be 1720, for instance, if it is between January 1st and March 24th, is really 1721.*

Your reference might look like this:

Archer v Yapp, Michaelmas 1833, 197

Go to the binder labelled C33 on the bookshelves and find the reference number for the volume you require (C 33/856). Key the reference into the computer terminal and when the Decree and Order Book arrives find the entry at 197. Find and summarise all the decrees and orders in the case before going on to other records. Once you know when the case started and appears to have finished, and you have some idea what it was all about, you are ready to look at the proceedings.

Chancery Proceedings, Masters' Reports and Certificates and Masters' Documents

Proceedings

The arguments presented by the lawyers for both sides are known as 'proceedings'. They are made up of bills, answers and other sorts of instruments which are in a number of different series, references C 1 - C 16 (Richard II to 1875) and J 54 (1876-1942).

Check through the lists of 'C' records in the *Public Record Office Guide* on the bookshelves to see which class you want; the records are simply described and the complicated range of name and topographical indexes are listed in *Courts of Equity,* a Guide to Chancery and other Legal Records, by Dorian Gerhold, (Newport, Isle of Wight, 1994) which you can buy in the PRO shop for £5. There is also a PRO information leaflet on Chancery proceedings (Equity suits) and a PRO readers' guide to Chancery records is in preparation.

Entry in Chancery Decree Book in Archer v Yapp, 17 Dec 1833. The case is dismissed.
(C 33/856 f)

Masters' Reports and Certificates

If the Decree and Order Books tell you that your case was referred to a Chancery Master for his opinion, as most were, then you should be able to find his report on the case among the records classified as C 38 and C 39 (J 57 from 1876).

The indexes to the reports have to be ordered on the computer. MORIS will tell you what the reference numbers for the indexes are if you key in the class number for the reports - C 38, etc.

The index will give you the folio or entry number for the books of reports. Go to the binders for C 38, C 39 or J 57 and find the reference number for the volume which contains your report; it might be C 38/312. Order it on the computer.

Masters' Documents

Once you have found the reports of the case, try the Masters' Documents; you may find there a great deal more about your squabbling ancestors than appears in the more official reports.

The documents are arranged in ten different series (C 117-126) filed under the name of the *last* master in each division. The office of master was abolished in

1852. You will know the name of the master to whom your case was referred from the entry in the Decree and Order Book. Ascertain the name of his last successor by consulting the note at the front of the catalogue of the class of records, C 103. This contains a succession list of masters in Chancery and an alphabetical list assigning masters to their divisions.

Once you have established which class of records you need, eg Master Tinney's Documents (C 120), ask MORIS what indexes exist by keying 'C 120' into the computer terminal. The indexes are the only means of reference for these documents; there are

Master Tinney's Documents   no class lists.

Other records

You may be able to add considerably to your Chancery story if there are extant depositions (evidence of witnesses, C 21 - C 24 and, from 1876, J 17) and/or affidavits (sworn statements, C 31 and, from 1876, J 90).

The exhibits produced in the course of litigation may be particularly exciting to the family historian as they are often personal items belonging to the parties concerned: letters, diaries, account books and sometimes even objects. Among the exhibits in the celebrated Tichborne case, where the identity of the heir to a baronetcy was in question, there are tiny pieces of still golden hair, carefully wrapped in tissue.

MORIS will tell you where indexes exist to these records.

Money in Chancery

There are stories in many families of vast fortunes waiting to be claimed 'in Chancery'. Most are, unfortunately, fairy tales and there is no crock of gold at the end of the search. There certainly are 'dormant funds', that is to say money in the custody of the court, usually deposited by solicitors who failed to locate beneficiaries in wills. There is a list published as a supplement to the *London Gazette*. Ask at the help desk in the Research Enquiries Room. If you are determined and have some documentation which proves your interest, you could try the Court Funds Office at 22 Kingsway, London WC2B 6LE. The office is open from 10 am to 4.30 pm and you can inspect the annually prepared accounts. Good hunting!

MAPS AND TITHE RECORDS

Maps and records described in this section are made available in the Map and Large Document Room on the second floor.

You can learn a lot about your ancestors' lives just by looking at a map of their area. The PRO has the largest map collection in the country. Large-scale Ordnance Survey maps are especially good - you may be able to spot your family's house and nearby churches, chapels, schools and places of work, like factories.

If your ancestors were country folk (in the nineteenth century), you really shouldn't miss the opportunity of looking at the relevant tithe map and apportionment, if one exists. The names of villagers (occupiers and tenants) and land owners are set out and you will probably be able to identify their farm or cottage on the map.

To find the reference for your tithe map and apportionment consult the binders labelled IR 29 and IR 30 and order what you want on the computer. They are arranged by county and then by tithe district. The apportionments and some of the maps are on film. You will find the following useful: *Maps for Family History*, William Foot (PRO Readers' Guide No. 9, 1994).

MARRIAGES - 'FLEET' AND OTHER IRREGULAR MARRIAGES IN LONDON

About twenty thousand marriages were conducted in various 'marriage shops' in London between 1667 and 1777. They were secret marriages performed in and around the Fleet prison, in other prisons and in the Mayfair Chapel, by clergy of low repute, for cash. Many of the marriages were bigamous, such as that of Alexander Selkirk, the model for the character of Robinson Crusoe. The Mayfair Chapel was patronized by the aristocracy and the others were mainly used by the lower ranks of society, especially sailors.

Other London marriage centres are listed in A Benton's *Irregular Marriage in London before 1754* (Society of Genealogists, 1993). You can buy it in the shop for £3.50.

Looking for a 'lost' marriage in the Fleet Registers

The collection is only partially indexed and a search of the many notebooks kept by Fleet parsons is likely to be a last resort after you have searched the IGI (see p 8), compilations of marriage licences and marriage indexes.

If either the bride or groom came from Kent, Surrey or Sussex you will find a name index in the binder which contains the catalogue of Fleet marriages, labelled RG 7 (in the lobby or Research Enquiries Room). A Hertfordshire index is in preparation. Some two thousand marriages (1709-1754) are listed in J S Burn's *The Fleet Registers* (London, 1833) and these are indexed in Boyd's Marriage Index which you can consult at the Society of Genealogists or the Guildhall Library.

To order a register you will need a three-part reference such as RG 7/92.

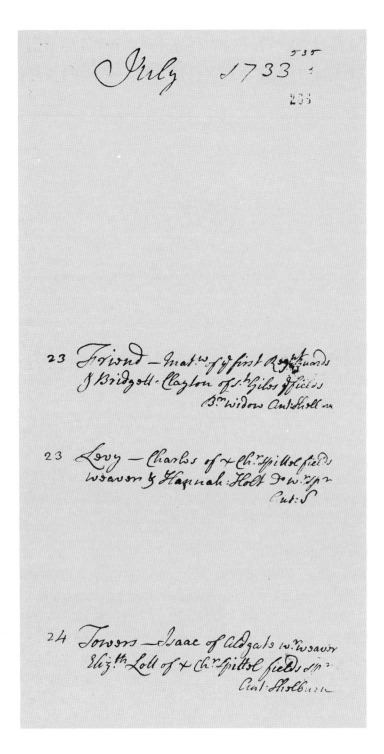

A soldier and two East London weavers marry in 'The Fleet', July 1733.
(RG 7/92 f.266)

MEDIEVAL ANCESTORS - BEFORE THE PARISH REGISTERS

For advice about medieval records go to the staff in the Map and Large Document Room on the second floor. Many of the records are in Latin.

Before the introduction of parish registers in 1538 and the recording of baptisms, marriages and burials, tracing ancestry with any degree of certainty is difficult unless you can link your family into a pedigree compiled by some herald or lawyer many years ago. There is a handful of sources. Most useful are wills (see p 113), manor court records and the records of the king's interference with his subjects through taxation, control of land transactions and the levying of feudal 'incidents' (obligations incident to feudal service, such as payment of aids and reliefs, or wardship of an heir).

Medieval ancestors

Manorial records

The country was, to a large extent, governed through the agency of local magnates who held courts where minor offences were tried. They were the major landowners and most ordinary people had cottages which they held from the lord of the manor by a form of tenure called copyhold.

Manorial records include details of locals committing misdemeanours and of

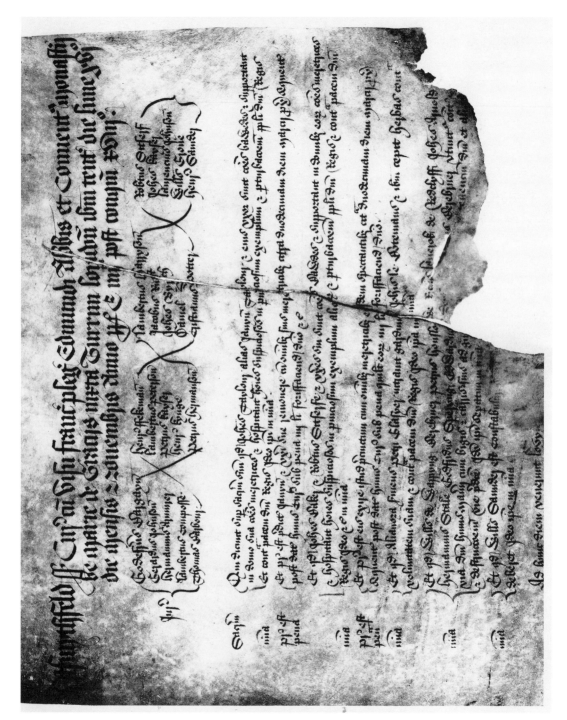

Court Roll for the Manor of East Smithfield, November 1478 (18 Edward IV). The manor belonged to the Abbot of St. Mary Graces, 'The Abbot of Tower Hill'. The jurors are listed and the first item concerns the keeping of a brothel. (SC 2/191 m2)

84

tenancy transactions. It was not only rural parts which came under the control of a lord of the manor. The Abbot of Tower Hill, as he was known, held a court where he prosecuted the prostitutes and gamblers who haunted the area around the Tower of London.

The manorial records in the PRO relate only to manors which were, at some stage, held by the crown. The best way to start a search for the manorial records for your family's area is to go to the Historical Manuscripts Commission (HMC) and National Register of Archives at Quality Court, Chancery Lane, London WC2A 1HP. There you can find out if anything survives for the area you are interested in and where the records now are; many are in local record offices. The HMC will answer queries sent to them by fax; their fax number is 0171 831 3550.

You may find the following useful: *Using Manorial Records*, Mary Ellis (PRO Readers' Guide No. 6, revised ed. 1997). It is available in the PRO shop and contains tables of regnal years from 1154-1837 which can be used to convert dates by year of reign, which are used in many of the lists of medieval records, to dates by calendar year. Another useful book is *My Ancestors were Manorial Tenants*, Peter B Park (SOG 2nd ed. 1994).

Finding medieval ancestors in the PRO

Apart from wills and court rolls, your best bet is to browse around in the Map and Large Document Room and go though the indexes to the 'calendars' of medieval government records. These volumes contain indexed abstracts of records produced by the Exchequer and the royal Chancery, the monarch's writing office - not to be confused with the Court of Chancery (see p 74) which grew out of it. The great rolls of the Chancery and Exchequer record grants of land and of office and make reference to ancestors of sufficient status to have direct dealings with the crown. The records which probably supply the most genealogical information are those known as Inquisitions Post Mortem (IPMs). These are the reports of investigations about the estates of people who held land directly from the crown; they give the names of heirs and widows. Proofs of age of under-age heirs are useful. There are various calendars of IPMs on the bookshelves.

Understanding medieval records

If you have no Latin your research will be very difficult and you are best advised to employ a qualified researcher to do it for you. Ask for a list of researchers at the enquiry desk.

If you have a grounding in Latin but are unfamiliar with medieval Latin you will need to refer to the *Medieval Latin Dictionary* which you will find on the bookshelves. E A Gooder's *Latin for Local Historians* (London, 1978) is also useful. You can buy it and Dennis Stuart's *Latin for Local and Family Historians* (Chichester, 1995) in the PRO shop. To help you understand the handwriting, buy *English Medieval Handwriting*, a Rycraft's Borthwick Wallet (York, 1973).

Records are dated by the sovereign's regnal year. To sort this out use the *Handbook of Dates* at the enquiry desk, or refer to Mary Ellis's *Using Manorial Records* (cited on p 85).

MERCHANT SEAMEN'S RECORDS

At present details of ordinary seamen in the Merchant Service are easily traceable in the PRO only between 1835 and 1854. For these years you can find a seaman's place and year of birth. During 1997-1998, records relating to 1913-1941 (registers in card index form) will be made available on microfiche in the record classes BT 348 - BT 350.

The records include Scotland. Many Irishmen served on British ships.

Seamen's careers

Until the mid-nineteenth century the Royal Navy and the Merchant Service recruited from the same labour force. Your seafaring ancestor may well have served in both and you may find him among the Admiralty records described on pp 104-107).

Researching the records at PRO Kew

Buy the following in the shop:

> *My Ancestor was a Merchant Seaman*, C J and M J Watts (Society of Genealogists, 2nd ed. 1991).

There are a variety of records that you can try; ask for a copy of the source sheet at the enquiry desk in the Research Enquiries Room.

The prime sources are on films which are read in the Microfilm Reading Room on the first floor. They are as follows:

1835-1844

Consult the binder for BT 112 in the Microfilm Reading Room; it is a list of alphabetically arranged registers of seamen. Select the register you want and note its reference number. Help yourself to the microfilm from the cabinet.

Wind on until you find your man; entries give name, age and birthplace.

1845-1854

Look in the binder for BT 114 in the Microfilm Reading Room; it contains an index to the registers of seamen's tickets (BT 113). Find your man and note his ticket number. Find that ticket number in the BT 114 list and note the three-part reference, such as BT 114/18 (18 is the item number **not** the ticket number). Help yourself to the film from the cabinet. Wind on until you find your entry; it will tell you where and when your seaman was born, the date of his first going to sea, the capacity he served in, his home address and whether or not he had served in the Royal Navy.

1845-1921 records of masters and mates only

Consult the catalogues of Masters and Mates' certificates of competency and service in the binders in the Microfilm Reading Room (BT 122-142). There are indexes for the period 1845-1894 in the class BT 127 on the shelves in the Research Enquiries Room. They can also be read on film in the Microfilm Reading Room. The certificates have to be ordered on the computer.

Crew Lists

Masters of merchant ships were obliged to keep muster rolls for each voyage recording the names of all sailors or men employed on board, their place of residence, where they joined the ship and the name of the ship on which they last sailed. Few survive earlier than 1800.

If you know when and where your ancestor might have taken ship you could try the muster rolls of the crews for those ports.

Find the ports in the binder for BT 98 in the lobby or Research Enquiries Room and order the musters you want on the computer.

After 1861

The PRO has only a sample of these (references BT 98 and BT 99). Check these first in case they include the list you want.

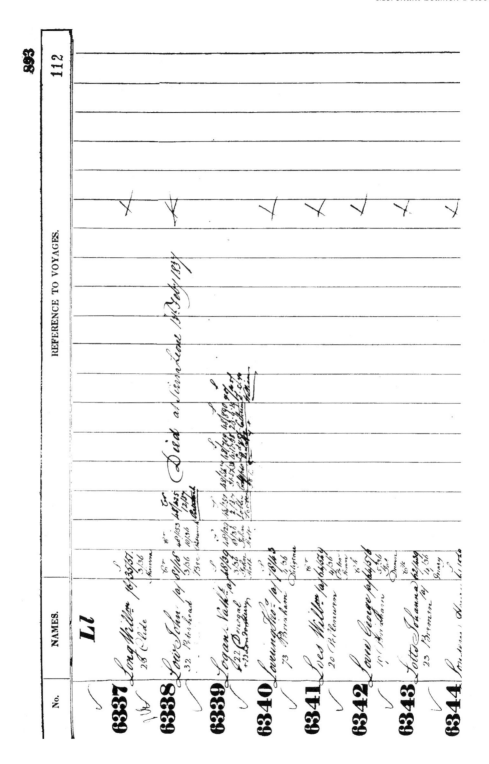

Extract from Register of Seamen, 1835-1844 'Li' to 'Lo'.   (BT 112/41)

Seamen's Records 1918-1974

Records of 250,000 seamen born after 1910 are being filmed and will be made available at PRO Kew in due course. These records are known as 'seamen's pouches' and contain individual papers such as identity cards, official correspondence and discharge papers. They were formerly in the custody of the Glamorgan County Record Office and there is no access to them at present.

The following are also to be transferred to the PRO in 1998-99:

- Indexes of mercantile marine medals for the First World War
- Indexes of certificate of competency (all deck officers), 1910-1930.

Sources outside the PRO

• Crew Lists 1861-1939

The National Maritime Museum, Romney Road, Greenwich, London SE10 9NF holds the crew lists for the years 1861 and 1862 and all years ending in 5.

The majority of crew lists for this period are in Newfoundland; searches are done for a fee. Write to: The Chairman, Maritime History Group, Memorial University of Newfoundland, St Johns, Newfoundland, Canada.

• Crew Lists and service records from 1939

These are retained by the Registrar General of Shipping and Seamen. Searches may be done for a fee. Write to: The Registrar General of Shipping and Seamen, Block 2, Government Buildings, St Agnes Road, Gabalfa, Cardiff CF4 4YA.

• Seamen's families, 1780-1854

The Trinity House Petitions (at the Society of Genealogists) are applications for relief from seamen's widows and dependants. There is a published index: *Trinity House Petitions* (Society of Genealogists, 1987).

NONCONFORMIST RECORDS, pre-1837

The 1851 ecclesiastical census shows that a quarter of the population were regular attendees at Nonconformist chapels. Chapel registers are a vital source for births/baptisms and burials for a large percentage of the population before central registration started in 1837. Marriages were also conducted in chapels before 1754. Some Nonconformist registers are held by local record offices, but the PRO holds several thousand registers; most are in the class RG 4 and may be read on film at the Family Records Centre. They are indexed on the IGI - so if you are at Kew you can check them out in the Microfilm Reading Room.

There is another, much smaller collection - *not indexed and not on film* - which you can read at Kew. These records are classified RG 8. Consult the binder for RG 8 in the lobby or Research Enquiries Room to see if there are any records for your family's denomination and/or area. Order the register for your chapel on the computer.

Registers of Quaker Monthly Meetings with birth and burial notes and original marriage certificates can also be read at Kew (reference RG 6). The indexes to these are alphabetical digests kept by the Society of Friends at Friends' House Library, Euston Road, London NW1 2BJ. You can research these and other records for a small fee.

See also under Cemetery Records, page 45.

You will find the following books most useful; buy them in the PRO shop:

My Ancestor was an English Presbyterian/Unitarian, Alan Rushton (SOG, 1993).

My Ancestors were Baptists, G R Breed (SOG, 1995).

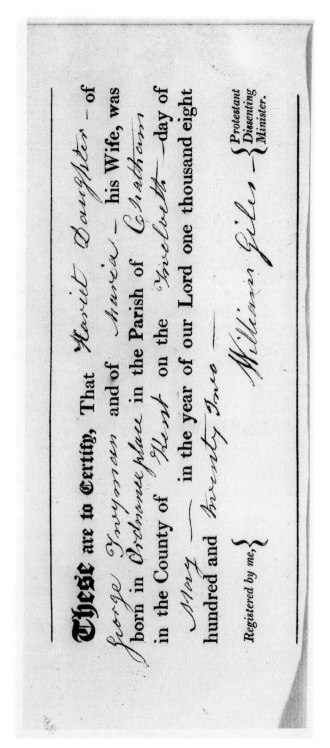

Entry of the birth of Hariet Twyman in the register of the Chatham Providence Chapel (Particular Baptists), 12 May 1822.   (RG 8/13)

My Ancestors were Congregationalists in England and Wales, D J H Clifford (SOG, 1992).

My Ancestors were Quakers, E H Milligan and M J Thomas (SOG, 1983).

Protestant Nonconformity and Roman Catholicism, David Shorney (PRO Readers' Guide No. 13, 1996).

NURSES' RECORDS

If you have a state registered nurse (SRN) or state enrolled nurse (SEN) in your family you should be able to find an entry for them in the registers of nurses from 1921 to 1983. There are three series:

Register of nurses (SRNs), 1921-1973 (reference DT 10, 201 volumes: indexes in DT 10/1-56)

Roll of assistant, later state enrolled nurses, 1944-1973 (reference DT 11, 51 volumes: indexes in DT 11/1-9)

Register of all nurses, 1973-1983 (DT 12, 28 volumes on fiche).

Using the catalogues labelled DT 10 and DT 11 (in the lobby or Research Enquiries Room), order the indexes which might refer to your nurse on the computer. When you have found her, send for the volume containing her entry. The entry will give: full name, address, place of training, maiden name if married at registration, details of marriages if married after registration, and there may be a date of death.

District nurses

For records of the associations which trained district nurses you should try the appropriate local record office and also write to the Director, Queen's Institute of District Nursing, 57 Lower Belgrave Street, London SW1.

There is a computerised index of hospital records in the PRO. Information from it will be given to you, but you should give a few days' notice. Telephone and ask for the Reader Services Department. A more up-to-date version is held by the Wellcome Institute for the History of Medicine, Wellcome Trust, 183 Euston Road, London NW1 2BP. Initial searches can be done on request by staff from the Contemporary Medical Archive Centre at the Wellcome Institute, tel. 0171 611 8483.

POLICE - LONDON METROPOLITAN AND ROYAL IRISH CONSTABULARY

The records of most police forces are either in local record offices or still with the forces concerned. If your ancestor served in a colonial force, you will have to apply to the country concerned, unless he was in the South African Constabulary between 1901 and 1908. (PRO reference CO 562, CO 639 and CO 640).

Metropolitan Police service records from 1829

The force was set up in 1829 and the PRO has service records from this date. It did *not* police the City of London. The City of London Police Records Office, 26 Old Jewry, London EC2R 8OJ, has full records from 1832.

1829-1836

Order item HO 65/26 on the computer. This is an alphabetical register of policemen, giving dates of promotion and demotion.

1830-1857, 1878-1933

There are five registers of recruits for these two periods. Consult the binder labelled MEPO 4 in the lobby or Research Enquiries Room. The item numbers for the registers are 333-338. Select the one you want and order it on the computer.

1889-1909

Certificates of service records are also in MEPO 4 as above. The item numbers are 361-447. Order the records on the computer.

Entries give date of birth, physical description, marital status, address, number of children, trade and last employer.

(4)

EXAMINATION

Of a CANDIDATE for the Situation of a Police Constable.

QUESTIONS.	ANSWERS.
Name	William George Kind
Age	27 years; born 9 day of Nov 18..
Height	5 feet 9¼ inches.
Weight	11 stones 4 lbs.
Chest measurement	34½ inches.
Complexion	Fresh
Eyes	Grey
Hair	Dark
Particular Marks	None
Where Born — In the Parish	Preston
Where Born — In or near the Town of	Brighton
Where Born — In the County of	Sussex
Trade or Calling	Coachman
Single or Married	Married
Number of Children	Two
Residence	149 Dennett Rd Croydon
What Public Services	
Police, Regiment, Corps, &c.	} none
Length of Service	
When discharged	
With whom last employed	W H Cole Esq
And where	The Lindens Beddington Lane Nr Croyd
If ever in the Metropolitan Police Service	No
Whether belonging to any illegal Secret Society	} No

Date 2nd February 189 7

A R Peachey
Examining Clerk.

SURGEON'S CERTIFICATE.

I HEREBY CERTIFY that I have examined the above Candidate, as to his health and bodily strength, and that I consider him fit for the Police Duty.

A O McK
Surgeon in Chief.

W B & L (788w)—41548—3000-7-94.

Examination of William George Kind, candidate for Metropolitan Police Constable, 1897. (MEPO 4/400)

1852-1932

Records of pensioners for this period are classified as MEPO 21. You will need to know roughly when your policeman retired. Consult the binder labelled MEPO 21; there is also a partial card index of names in the Research Enquiries Room.

1932 to date

Pension records for this period are kept at the Metropolitan Police Office, F4 Branch Police Pensions, 2 Bessborough Street, London SW1V 2JF.

Royal Irish Constabulary (RIC)

This force policed the whole of Ireland except Dublin between 1836 and 1922.

The prime source for RIC personnel is classified as HO 184. Consult the indexes and registers to HO 184 in the Research Enquiries Room (MORIS the computerized guide to means of reference will tell you where they are) and then get the three-part reference you need from the binder labelled HO 184 in the lobby or Research Enquiries Room. Order your records on the computer.

Entries give name, age, height, religion, trade and marital status and nationality of officers and their wives.

RAILWAY WORKERS PRE-NATIONALIZATION

There were hundreds of railway companies and thousands of our ancestors were employed by them. Survival of staff records, unfortunately, is very patchy; there is much more for the Great Western Railway than for any of the others. Before you start your research you are advised to consult the following book in the Research Enquiries Room (MORIS will tell you where it is) or you can buy it in the shop:

David Hawkings, *Railway Ancestors* (Stroud, 1995)

It lists all the companies and their surviving records and explains in what series you might find a fireman, engine driver, porter etc.

If you are not sure which company your ancestor worked for, but you know which station or area he worked in, you could look at *The British Railway Atlas, the last days of the Big Four* (1947, reprinted 1987); it is also in the Research Enquiries Room.

Having identified which class of records you need to look at from David Hawkings' book, go to the binders with RAIL labels on them in the lobby or Research Enquiries Room and order the records you need on the computer. You may have to go through a large number of registers, so make sure you order three items and then three more as soon as the original three have been delivered to you.

London Brighton & South Coast Railway
Register of Appointments

1860 No	Date of Appointment	Name		Occupation	Station
599	1.12.60	Kidgell	O	Porter	Streatham
600	1.12.60	Edames	E.S.	Gateman	Chichester
601	1.12.60	Pincott	W.	Porter	Epsom
602	1.10.60	Haybittel	H.	Carter	Battersea
603	19.11.60	Blackaller	J	Night Watchman	Brighton Gds
604	1.12.60	Matthews	J	Del Porter	London
605	1.12.60	Stringer	H.	Messenger	Brixton
606	1.12.60	Holden	C.	Messenger	Brighton Sds
607	1.12.60	Taylor	W.	Goods Porter	Brighton
608	1.12.60	Soan	C.	Clerk	Brighton Sds
609	1.12.60	Edwards	F.	Clerk	Brighton
610					
611	1.12.60	Evans	C.J.	Messenger	Brighton Gds
612	1.12.60	Morris	G.	Carman	Brighton
613	1.12.60	Chevis	J	Porter	Brighton
614	1.12.60	Haybittle	A.	Carter	Brighton
615	1.12.60	Martin	B.	Carter	Brighton
616	9.12.60	Linard	J	Carl Lad	London Bge
617	1.12.60	Teual	B.	Clerk	Brighton Sds
618	1.12.60	Cole	W.	Porter	Brighton
619	15.12.60	Cullum	G.	Porter	Norwood
620	14.12.60	Phillips	J.	Porter	Sutton
621	5.11.60	Bond	H.	Clerk	Eastbourne
622	20.12.60	Richardson	J	Clerk	Battersea
623	24.12.60	Stander	C.	Carman	St Leonards
624	23.7.60	Best	S.	Porter	Brighton Gds
625	14.12.60	Frill	J	Carman	Brighton
626	14.12.60	Cannard	J	Carman	Brighton
627	14.12.60	Hill	G	Porter	Brighton
628	14.12.60	Rowland	D	Carman	Brighton

Entries from the London Brighton and South Coast Railway Register of Appointments, 1860. (RAIL 414/760) Reproduced by permission of the British Railways Board.

ROYAL AIR FORCE
SERVICE RECORDS

Most Royal Air Force personnel records are held by the Ministry of Defence. Write to MOD PMC , RAF Innsworth, Gloucester GL3 1EZ. Write to section PM (AR)1b (RAF) for officers (discharged after 1920) and to section P Man 3d (RAF) for airmen.

At PRO Kew

There are some service records for the RAF's predecessor the Royal Flying Corps (founded in 1911) among the First World War Army service records described on p 39. They relate only to men who left the service before the RAF was founded on 1 April 1918.

Records of RAF medals are in the class AIR 2. Consult the binder for AIR 2 in the lobby or Research Enquiries Room and find the section: code B 30. This contains recommendations for awards. Order your record on the computer. I I Taverner, *The Distinguished Flying Medal: a record of courage 1918-1982*, (Polstead, 1990) gives a list of recipients of the DFM.

A complete muster of the RAF on 1 April 1918 exists. There are two copies of it: references AIR 1/819 and AIR 10/232-237. Order them on the computer.

Officers' careers can be traced in outline from the *Air Force List* on the bookshelves at the far end of the Microfilm Reading Room. A confidential list, with information not included in the normal list, was published between 1939 and 1954. These volumes have to be ordered on the computer, references AIR 10/3814-3840, 5237-5256, 5413, 5581-5582. Consult the binders for AIR 10 in the lobby or Research Enquiries Room to get the volume you want.

The record books of officers' services, 1918-1920, can be read on film in the Microfilm Reading Room. Although the books were started in 1918, they have retrospective entries. Records of most officers discharged or killed in action during the First World War and to 1920 may be found. Addresses, names of next-of-kin or wife, date of birth and units served in are listed.

Find the binder labelled AIR 76 on top of the microfilm cabinet and identify the item you need: it might be AIR 76/347 Mill, Arthur to Miller J A R F. Help yourself to the film from the cabinet.

Operational records and more about RAF personnel are described in the essential guide:

RAF Records in the PRO, S Fowler, P Elliott, R Conyers Nesbit, C Goulter (PRO Readers' Guide No. 8, 1994) available in the shop.

ROYAL MARINES' SERVICE RECORDS

If your ancestor served in the Marines before 1918 (the force of 'sea soldiers' was set up first in 1664 and permanently established under the Admiralty authority in 1755), you have a good chance of finding him in the PRO.

Consult *Records of the Royal Marines* by Garth Thomas, (PRO Readers' Guide No. 10, 1994), or buy it in the shop.

Other ranks

1664-1789

Description books, arranged by division and company, are classified as ADM 158.

1790-1901

Look your ancestor up in the alphabetical card index of attestation papers (discharge documents) in the Research Enquiries Room. Using the information found on the card order the original attestation paper on the computer. Do this by referring to the binder labelled ADM 157 in the same room. You will need a three-part reference such as ADM 157/88.

1884-1918

For service records consult the binder labelled ADM 313 in the Research Enquiries Room or lobby. Indexes to service records are items 27-109. Find your marine and then refer to the binder for ADM 159 which is the catalogue of service records. Order his record on the computer. There is also an index to service records in the Research Enquiries Room. Entries give date and place of birth, trade, religion, physical description and career details.

Officers

No original records of service for Royal Marine officers appointed before 1793 have survived.

Check through the entries for your officer in the published *Navy List* from 1797; the PRO's set is at the far end of the Microfilm Reading Room.

Now look your officer up in the card index to officers' service records in the Research Enquiries Room (officers appointed before 1915). This is a card index to Royal Naval and Royal Marine officers.

Using the information found in the card index, refer to the binder labelled ADM 196 in the same room. The class ADM 196 is the main series of records for naval officers (including Royal Marine officers) who were appointed from the mid-eighteenth century to 1915.

After 1915 (officers) and 1918 (other ranks)

For information from officers' service records after 1915 write to: The Commandant General, Royal Marines, Ministry of Defence (Navy), Whitehall, London SW1A 2HB.

For information from the service records of other ranks who enlisted less than 75 years ago, write to: Drafting and Record Office, Royal Marines, HMS *Centurion*, Grange Road, Gosport, Hants PO13 9XA.

THE ROYAL NAVY

- *Tracing a sailor before 1853 may be difficult unless you have the name of a ship on which he served.*

- *If your sailor was serving in 1861 you might like to start the search by looking in the index of seamen in the 1861 census at the Family Records Centre. Here are listed all seamen on ships both in home waters and abroad on census night.*

Naval records tend to be fragmentary; they are most useful to the family historian after the introduction of continuous service engagement in 1853. After this date, and perhaps before, you will be able to find out where he sailed, the ships he served in, what his promotions and punishments were, what he looked like and something about his family.

Before 1853 the Royal Navy and Merchant Navy tended to recruit seamen from the same pool of labour and there was no such thing as 'joining the Navy' as a career, except for officers. Thus Obadiah Archer, living in Wapping (London's 'sailortown'), might have been recruited (in a local tavern) by the captain of a naval vessel who was going to fight with Nelson at Trafalgar. Once the campaign was over he would have been paid off and perhaps joined the crew of an East Indiaman going to collect spices and silks from the sub-continent.

The Navy was divided into:

- ratings (ordinary seamen)

- warrant officers (men with specialist jobs like boatswains or gunners)

- officers

Records at PRO Kew

Ratings and warrant officers

Start with the records listed below and then consult Nicholas Rodger's *Naval Records for Genealogists* (HMSO, 1988) to find other lines of research. You can read it in the Research Enquiries Room.

1688-1798

Ships' Muster Books: no name indexes - you need to know the name of the ship on which your ancestor served.

Musters list the crew and sometimes give age and place of birth.

To find the muster for your ship consult the binder for ADM 36 - ADM 39 in the lobby or Research Enquiries Room.

1802-1919

Pensioned seamen only.

The records classified as ADM 29 give a brief service record for seamen who received a pension; before 1834 they were almost all warrant officers.

For 1802-1868 there is card index of names in the Research Enquiries Room.

To look at the original documents, consult the binder labelled ADM 29 in the lobby or Research Enquiries Room. Order your record on the computer using a three-part reference, such as ADM 29/100.

1853-1872

Continuous Service Engagement Books; all seamen.

Find your seaman in the indexes on the bookshelves in the Microfilm Reading Room. Then refer to the binder labelled ADM 139 in the same room. Order your record on the computer.

Service record of Robert Gillies, Engine Room Artificer in the Royal Navy.
(ADM 188/107/96242)

Entries give place of birth, physical description and summary of service.

1837-1891

Seamen's Services; all seamen.

Find your seaman in the indexes to Seamen's Services on the bookshelves in the Microfilm Reading Room and note his number. Then go to the binder labelled ADM 188 in the same room and find the three-part reference for the record you want, eg ADM 188/5.

Entries give date of birth and enlistment, first ship and period of service.

Chaplains

There is a card index of chaplains (taken from the class ADM 6) in the Research Enquiries Room.

Officers

Trace an outline of your ancestor's career (lieutenant upwards) from the published *Navy List* (from 1782) and naval biographies on the bookshelves in the Microfilm Reading Room and the Library.

Service records from 1756:

There are card indexes to officers' service records (ADM 196) in the Research Enquiries Room in several different series; make sure you have the right one. To order the register you need to consult the binder labelled ADM 196 in the same room. Order the register on the computer using a three-part reference such as ADM 196/38.

Find the entry for your officer in the register. From the mid-nineteenth century personal details are usually given: place and date of birth, marriage and death. The commanding officer's opinion of your ancestor may be revealed in the summary of his confidential report.

There are a number of other categories of records which may help in your hunt for a naval officer; see Appendix I of *Naval Records for Family Historians*.

Naval wills

Do not forget to look for a will or grant of administration for your seafaring ancestor. Sailors had to make legal arrangements for the disposal of their outstanding pay after death, so there exist many thousands of wills and administrations (grants made in cases of intestacy) for ordinary seamen as well as officers.

Wills are to be found in the records of the ordinary probate courts (see pp 113 to 124). Copies of wills and grants of administration were also kept by the Admiralty:

1786-1882 ratings:	ADM 48, indexed in ADM 142
1800-1860 ratings:	ADM 44, indexed in ADM 141
1830-1860 officers:	ADM 45, indexed in part; cards in the Research Enquiries Room.

First World War and since

At the MOD

Most of the service records of ratings who enlisted after 1891 and of officers who joined from the 1880s are not yet in the PRO. The records, or what survives of them, are due to be made available in the PRO within the next two years.

For information up to 1939 (for a fee) from them, write to: The Ministry of Defence, CS(R)2a, Bourne Avenue, Hayes, Middlesex UB3 1RS.

For records from 1939 write to PP1 A1, HMS *Centurion*, Grange Road, Gosport, Hants PO13 9XA.

In the PRO

Medals. Recipients of the *British War Medal, Victory Medal* and the *Star* are listed in the binder for ADM 171 at items 89-131. Help yourself to the appropriate film in the Microfilm Reading Room. No details are given beyond name and service number but the latter is useful if you are writing to the MOD for information.

Navy List **for officers**. The PRO's set is in the Microfilm Reading Room.

Casualties. There is a card index in the Research Enquiries Room of all officers, warrant officers and midshipmen who died 1914-1920. The cards give name, rank, date and cause of death. The next of kin can be found in the registers ADM 242/7-10; order these on the computer. Other casualty records are in ADM 104.

Pensions (mainly to officers' widows). These records are classified as PMG and there are detailed listings in *Naval Records for Genealogists*.

Ships' Logs. If you know which ship your seaman served on, you can find out where it sailed and the engagements in which it was involved. Officers may be mentioned by name. Ships' logs are in the class ADM 53; submarine logs are in ADM 173. There is a useful card index of ships and submarines in the Second World War in the Research Enquiries Room.

For other suggestions see Jack Cantwell's *The Second World War: A guide to documents in the Public Record Office* (HMSO, 1993).

TAX LISTS

Tax lists will not provide genealogical data as such but may give an indication of your ancestor's financial status. Also, if you know or suspect that your ancestors lived in a particular place their presence on a tax list will confirm this.

Land Tax records, which can be very useful for the eighteenth and early nineteenth centuries, are mainly held in local record offices. The PRO holds an important nationwide series for 1798 (reference IR 23), which lists all occupiers and owners of property in England and Wales subject to Land Tax at that date. It is arranged by Land Tax parishes within counties. Window Tax records are mainly held locally.

Medieval to eighteenth century: 'lay subsidies'

Find the catalogue labelled E 179 (Lay Subsidies) in the Research Enquiries Room. These list surviving records of the payment of a number of taxes.

Where the lay subsidy records include lists of *names of taxpayers* (as opposed to just numbers of people with tax liability), this is noted in the margin of the E 179 catalogue. The arrangement is by county in 'hundreds', and date. Go through the catalogue and see if there is anything for your family's village or town.

The records of the Hearth Tax are probably the most useful.

Finding your ancestors in the Hearth Tax, 1662-1674

Charles II's unpopular tax 'Chimney money' demanded payment into the Exchequer of two shillings a year on every fireplace. The records provide lists of tax payers (heads of households) with the number of hearths for which each was responsible. This is a clue to status; ordinary folk only had one or two and the gentry might have ten! Some lists of exemptions also survive within these records. The tax was widely evaded, so if your family don't appear on the list it doesn't necessarily mean they weren't there.

Unless the records are published (many are, on a county basis, see below) you will need to know whereabouts your ancestors lived. The records are arranged by 'hundreds' so you will have to find out which 'hundred' the village or town was in. Do this by consulting Lewis's *Topographical Dictionary* (MORIS will tell you where to find it).

Check first that the records for your area have not been published, by reference to Jeremy Gibson's *Hearth Tax and Other Later Stuart Tax Lists and the Association Oath Rolls* (Federation of Family History Societies, 2nd ed, 1996, kept behind the desk in the Research Enquiries Room). If there is a publication ask MORIS if the PRO has a copy and where you can read it.

If there is no published version, or if you would like to look at the original version anyway, go through the E 179 catalogue and find your county (and perhaps hundred). Individual places are not listed in the catalogue except for major towns. Order the tax list on the computer using a four-part reference such as E 179/244/15.

Hearth Tax List for Earl's Court, 1673-4 (25/26 Charles II). (E 179/143/370)

Records of the Valuation Office, 1909-1915: the 'Field Books'

These records (reference IR 58), associated with the levying of tax on property, provide *a countrywide list of most properties in England and Wales.* Names of owners and tenants are given and sometimes occupiers, along with a detailed description of the property. If you want to find out what sort of house your family lived in and who their landlord was, the Field Books will tell you. They will also, of course, confirm that your family were living where you thought they were!

There are no name indexes and the means of reference are very complicated. You would be well advised to consult William Foot's *Maps for Family History* (PRO Readers' Guide No. 9, 1994).

Go up to the Map and Large Document Room on the second floor and ask for help. The Field Books will be delivered to you in there.

WILLS AND PROBATE RECORDS

The PRO's PCC wills and grants of administration (made in some cases of intestacy) 1383-1858, may be consulted on film both at PRO Kew (in the Microfilm Reading Room) and at the Family Records Centre in Myddelton Street, Islington. Other probate records can be read only at PRO Kew.

Are all English and Welsh wills in the PRO?

No. Officially registered wills are distributed thus:

Wills proved from January 1858:

> in Somerset House (copies of *all* wills).
> in District Probate Registries (locally proved wills only).

Wills proved before January 1858:

> in the PRO (some, see below).
> in local record offices (some, see below).

Before 1858 there were hundreds of probate courts, most of them church courts. The wills in the PRO are those which were proved (ie given the stamp of authority) by the most senior court in the south of England, the Prerogative Court of the Archbishop of Canterbury (PCC).

PCC wills go back to the fourteenth century. Most of the early ones are those of rich and titled people; the later ones come from all ranks of society. Wills of people of small means, by and large, tended to go the minor courts, however, and are now mainly in local record offices.

Jeremy Gibson's *Probate Jurisdictions: Where to Look for Wills* (Federation of Family History Societies, 4th ed, 1994) is a comprehensive guide to the location of wills in local record offices and elsewhere. You can consult it in the Microfilm Reading Room or buy it in the shop.

What are the chances of finding a will for your ancestor in the PRO?

Firstly, remember he or she has to have died before 1858. The richer he was, the more likely it is that you will be successful in your search, but there are many thousands of PCC wills for quite humble people, especially in the nineteenth century. It is probably best to start a will search with the wills deposited in local record offices; the Gibson guide cited above will tell you where to go. For the period 1796-1858 the Death Duty indexes (described on pp 59-61) may be a help in finding out where your ancestor's will now is.

There are more southerners than northerners in the PCC. If your rich ancestor lived in the north of England, unless he had investments in the south, his will would probably have been proved in the court of the Archbishop of York (Prerogative Court of York: PCY) and will now be in the Borthwick Institute of Historical Research at St Anthony's Hall, Peasholme Green, York YO1 2PW. Tel: 01904 59861 x 274.

The ruling before 1858 was that anyone who died with personal estate (goods, cash, leases, investments etc - *not freehold or copyhold property*) to the value of £5 (£10 in London) in more than one diocese had to have their estate dealt with by the archbishop's court. This ruling ceased to be strictly observed and by the 1830s the PCC was handling one third of all the country's probate business.

Thus one might expect to find the will of a seventeenth or eighteenth-century yeoman farmer proved in a minor court (and now in a local record office) but could reasonably expect to find the will of his nineteenth-century equivalent in the PCC at the PRO.

English and Welsh people who died abroad, including poor sailors, had their wills proved in the PCC, as did anyone who had personal estate both at home and abroad (like new emigrants to North America, for instance).

Did your ancestor leave a will at all?

Only a small percentage of the male population left wills which went to probate, before the present century, perhaps five per cent. Fewer women left wills; married women's property was usually disposed of by their husbands and spinsters were often too poor to bother with any official bequests.

If a man died intestate, ie, without leaving a will, there *might* be a grant of administration made on his estate. Such grants were made only if the estate was considerable or there were some special circumstances.

Grants of Administration

In some cases, if a man died without leaving a will ('intestate'), the court would make a grant of administration to his next-of-kin or wife. Usually these grants were only made if:

the deceased was wealthy;

there was some need for a legal title to be established. One of the most usual circumstances was that someone who was owed money by the deceased applied to administer his estate - that being the surest way of getting his hands on what was owed to him; or

the widow or next-of-kin thought that there was someone else who might make a claim on the estate.

The main records of PCC grants of administration are brief entries in a series of registers called 'Administration Act Books' (reference PROB 6); special grants are entered in separate registers called 'Act Books: Limited Administrations' (reference PROB 7). See p 119 for a description of how they are indexed and what they contain.

How to find a will in the PRO

You will find the following work useful for finding your way round PCC wills and administrations: *Prerogative Court of Canterbury Wills and Other Probate Records*, Miriam Scott (PRO Readers' Guide No. 15, 1997).

All registered wills (court copies) are on microfilm and the class code for them is PROB 11. You will need an approximate date of death.

The numbers in the will indexes refer to 16-page gatherings in the will registers; they are not page or folio numbers.

1383-1800

For this period there is a series of printed indexes in the Microfilm Reading Room (MORIS or the staff will tell you where they are). Note the year and the number given in the index; this is the gathering or quire number.

Now find the binder labelled PROB 11; turn to the part of the catalogue which relates to your year and quire number. You will need a three-part number to find the film, such as PROB 11/56. When you have got the film with this reference on it, refer back to the quire number.

Suppose the index has shown you that Joshua Archer's will was proved in 1667 and the quire number is 19. The catalogue labelled PROB 11 shows that the wills proved in 1667 entered in the quire numbers 1-50 have the PRO reference PROB 11/345. Make a note of the reference PROB 11/345/19 and go to the film cabinet and take out the film numbered PROB 11/345. Take it to a microfilm reader and wind on until you find quire number 19 (the large number at the top right hand side). The quire number appears every 16 pages. *Ignore the stamped or manuscript numbers which appear on every page.* Joshua Archer's will is entered somewhere among the 16 pages following the page which has a large 19 on the top right-hand corner.

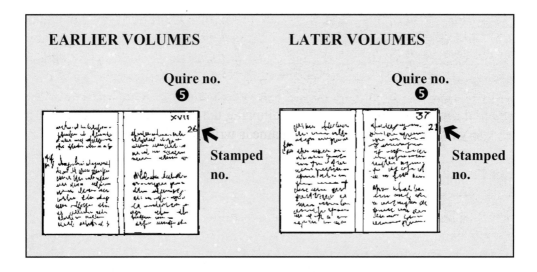

1800-1858

For this period there are annual manuscript indexes which you can consult on film.

Look at the binder labelled PROB 12 and find the annual index volume for wills. Help yourself to the film and wind on until you have found the right part of the alphabet. They are not in strict alphabetical order; you may have to go through all the 'A's to find John Archer's will, for instance.

The indexes are both to wills and grants of administration, so make sure you have got the right sort of grant. There are headings to guide you; for the most part administration entries have a month by them and no number.

When you have found your man, note the year of probate and the number by the entry. It refers to a 16-page gathering or quire in the will register.

Go to the binder labelled PROB 11 on the bookshelves and find the section which relates to the wills proved in your probate year. Note the reference number for the quire which includes yours.

Thus you have found that John Archer of Essex left a will which was proved in 1805 and registered at gathering 321. The PROB 11 catalogue tells you that wills registered in 1801 at quires 300-400 bear the reference PROB 11/925.

Take film PROB 11/925 from the cabinet, put it on a microfilm reader and wind on until you get to quire number 321. The quire number appears every 16 pages at the very top right-hand corner. *Ignore the stamped or manuscript numbers which appear on every frame* unless you wish to place an order for a copy in which case you will need to note the *stamped* numbers. John Archer's will is entered somewhere in the 16 pages following the one which has a large 321 in the very top right-hand corner. His name is written in the margin.

Buying a copy of the will

Wills can be long, complicated and very informative, so you will probably want a copy of your will to take home and ponder over.

Self-service copy cards are available from the enquiry desk. Ask the staff to show you how the reader printer works, if you get stuck.

Understanding the will

If you have difficulty with the odd word, the staff will help. If you are at a loss with the whole thing, take a copy and your local family history society may help, or you can get the name of a professional researcher from the enquiry desk.

The £2.50 booklet *Wills, Probate and Death Duty Records* by Jane Cox (Federation of Family History Societies, 1993) has a glossary of probate terms and other useful information. You can buy it in the shop.

It is important that you bear the following points in mind:

> *landed property was often disposed of by other means than wills eg marriage settlements;*
>
> *children might have their inheritance settled on them at marriage or at 21 - so not all children are necessarily mentioned in a will;*
>
> *wills could take a long time to be proved, years sometimes, so search the indexes forward from the date of death;*
>
> *the probate clause written at the foot of the will (in Latin until 1733) tells you the name of the person who carried out the terms of the will. It will not always be the executor or executrix appointed in the will; he or she may be dead or not available.*

You have read the will - are there any other records which relate to it?

For many PCC wills there are supporting documents of one sort and another. These are listed in Miriam Scott's book, cited above. The most useful are:

- inventories (see p 122)
- Death Duty records (see pp 59-62)
- records of lawsuits about wills.

Records of lawsuits

If the will indexes show that the will was proved 'by sent[ence]' or 'by decr[ee]', it often means there was a fight over the estate and there may be a great deal of surviving documentation. The evidence given by witnesses (called 'depositions' or 'cause papers') is usually the most interesting and informative.

It often happens that if a will was in dispute in the probate court there was also a suit in the Court of Chancery, which had a different sort of jurisdiction. See pp 74 to 79; for the late seventeenth century see Peter Coldham's *Indexes to disputed wills in Chancery.* MORIS or a member of staff will tell you where it is.

The records of lawsuits are not on film. The outline of a case can be constructed from the Acts of Court Books (PROB 29) and the Acts of Court (PROB 30). PROB 29 volumes have integral indexes, but the early indexes are by plaintiff, not by deceased. The evidence and witnesses are in the classes PROB 24 (integral indexes in volumes), PROB 26, PROB 28, PROB 31, PROB 37. Consult the binders labelled PROB and order the records you want to read on the computer.

How to find a grant of administration

Records of PCC ordinary intestacy grants or grants of administration (abbreviated to 'admons') are on film and may be read *in the Microfilm Reading Room at PRO Kew and in the Family Records Centre at Myddelton Street. Limited and special grants (the index indicates if grants were of this nature) can be read only at PRO Kew.*

There are published indexes on the bookshelves only for the years 1559-1663. For the period 1664-1858 you will have to use the yearly manuscript indexes which are not in strict alphabetical order. These are on film; find out which film you want from the binder labelled PROB 12 and help yourself to the film from the cabinet. Having found your man, note the *year, month and county* of the entry.

Turn to the catalogue of Administration Act Books (in a binder labelled PROB 6) and find the reference for the Act Book for the year in which your grant was made. You need a three-part reference, such as PRO 6/217, to identify the film.

Help yourself to the film from the cabinet and put it on to a reader. The entries are arranged by month before 1744, but there are subsections within each month, so make sure you check all through.

From 1744 the Act Books are arranged in five divisions called 'seats'. Four of them are county sections. Section three, for instance, contains grants for intestates from Derbyshire, Gloucestershire and eleven other counties. The first section (the 'Registrars' Seat') should always be checked as it contains, amongst other things, all grants made following litigation and thus relates to people who lived all over the country.

The seat arrangement is given below.

Bedford	4	Norfolk	4
Berkshire	4	Northampton	3
Bristol	2 & 3	North Britain	1
Buckinghamshire	4	Northumberland	1
Cambridgeshire	4	Nottingham	1
Carlisle	1	Oxford	3
Chester	1	P.T.S. (Abroad)	1
City of London	5	Rutlandshire	3
Cornwall	2	Shropshire	3
Cumberland	1	Sunderland	2
Derbyshire	3	Somersetshire	2
Devonshire	2	Southampton	2
Dorsetshire	2	Staffordshire	3
Durham	1	Suffolk	4
Essex	4	Surrey	2
Gloucestershire	3	Sussex	2
Herefordshire	3	Wales	3
Hertfordshire	4	Warwickshire	3
Huntingdonshire	4	Wiltshire	2
Ireland	1	Worcestershire	3
Kent	1	York (The County and entire province)	1
Lancashire	1		
Leicestershire	3	Grants on Litigated Estates (by decree)	1
Lincolnshire	4		
London	5	Outlying London Parishes (Middlesex)	4
Middlesex	4 & 5		

Understanding the grant

The wording of all grants follows the same pattern and, even though they are in Latin before 1733, it is simple to extract the information you want.

The name in the margin is that of the dead man. The first thing noted in the body of the entry is the date, then follows the name of the grantee (wife, next-of-kin or creditor), then his/her relationship to the deceased and the latter's address.

From 1796 the value of the personal estate is given in the margin. This *excludes copyhold and freehold land.*

A sample translation is given below.

Richus Swifte ad de bonis commis'mensis Martii 1617	Decimo quarto die emanavit comissio Francisce Swift relte Richi Swift nuper parochie beate Marie Magdalene in Barmondsey Com Surr' des' hentes etc. ad administranda bona iura et credita dci des' de bene etc. in persona Richi Goodall notarii publici procuris sui etc. iurat'	Winton

Ascensio in Inventarium exhibitum xxj

Blasii Computavit |
| Richard Swifte admon of goods unadministered granted March 1617/8 | On the fourteenth day [of March] a commission issued to Frances Swift the relict of Richard Swifte of the parish of the Blessed Mary Magdalene in Bermondsey in the county of Surrey deceased having etc [whilst he lived and at the time of his death goods etc. sufficient to found the jurisdiction of the Prerogative Court] to administer the goods rights and credits of the said deceased she being sworn truly to administer in the person of her proctor, Richard Goodall, notary public | Winchester diocese

Inventory to be exhibited by Ascension; exhibited on [March] 21st

Account to be returned by the feast of St Blaise (February); [administrator] has accounted |

Entry in Administration Act Book, 1598/9 (PROB 6/6, f.9) The left-hand marginal note indicates that a 'de bonis' grant was made nineteen years after the original grant. Richard Swifte's widow had evidently died without administering her husband's estate.

There is an entry for my ancestor in the administration indexes but I cannot find it on the PROB 6 film!

Either you are looking in the wrong 'seat' (see p 120) or your grant is 'special' or 'limited'. The index should indicate if the grant was of this nature. Special and limited grants are described in detail in Cox, *Wills, Inventories and Death Duties.*

Before 1810 special and limited grants were entered in the same registers as ordinary grants; they are easily recognizable as they are much longer than the ordinary entries. From 1810 they were entered in a separate series of registers called Limited Administration Act Books (PROB 7). *These are not on film.* Consult the binder labelled PROB 7 and order the volume you want on the computer. It will be delivered to the Document Reading Room. The arrangement of grants in the books is the same as that given on p 121.

There is not much information in the Act Book entry - is there anything to supplement it?

Inventories

A list of the deceased's belongings (inventory) may survive; this is most likely for the period 1666-c.1730, but it is worth checking through the binders labelled PROB 31 PCC Exhibits, Main Series, 1722-1858 (in the Research Enquiries Room), and the Series II inventories in the class PROB 3, 1702 and 1718-1782. The earlier inventories are listed in detail and indexed; they are in the binders labelled PROB 4, PROB 5, PROB 32.

Bonds

Administration bonds survive for the period 1714-1858. Bonds give an indication of the value of the estate and the name and address of the administrator and the person who stood security for him. Consult the binder for PROB 46. Bonds are arranged in bundles according to date/seat of the grant to which they relate.

Death Duty Records

These are the most useful source for supplementing Administration Act Books. Those for 1796-1857 are seen on microfilm at the Family Records Centre.

Those for 1858-1903 are stored away from Kew and so five days' notice must be given before they can be seen.

They are described on pp 59 to 62. The later volumes 1858-1903 supplement the information found in grants of administration in the Principal Registry of the Family Division at Somerset House.

Lawsuits

If there was litigation over the estate, pleadings and evidences may survive (see p 79).

Codicil to Nell Gwynne's will giving £5 to 'Orange Nan'; it was the subject of litigation. (PROB 20/1141)

My search for a will or grant of administration has not been successful - what shall I do now?

The three most usual reasons why you have not found a will/admon are:

1. No grant was ever made - very common among the poor. Few agricultural labourers left wills and for even fewer were there grants of administration. Most of them held their cottages by a form of land tenure called 'copyhold' which passed at death to the heir or widow. The record of the surrender to the lord of the manor and regrant to the heir or widow was entered on the manor court roll, which you might be able to find (see pp 83-85). Copyhold was abolished in 1926.

2. You have not searched for a long enough period - search on a few more years.

3. The grant was made in the Prerogative Court of York or one of the minor courts. Check the printed indexes of wills proved in other courts, which you will find on the bookshelves (MORIS will help), and the Death Duty indexes (IR 27) as described on pp 59-61. If you know which county/area your ancestor died in it is probably best to go to the county/local record office. To find out where you need to go, consult Jeremy Gibson's *Probate Jurisdictions: Where to look for Wills* (cited above).

POSTSCRIPT

In the age of microform and the Internet, CD-ROM and immediate access to data, it is easy for us family historians to forget that we are engaged in the gentle business of historical research. There are no quick and easy answers (though it sometimes feels as if there are); the evidence has to be sifted and considered and the story pursued up side alleys and along unlikely by-ways. It is, what is more, research of the most exacting nature. Ordinary historians are, by and large, looking for great bulks of evidence and sweeps of events. Family historians have a far more difficult task; they are looking for specific, minor events and, for the most part, ordinary people who have only left the slightest account of themselves. Contrary to popular belief, a far deeper understanding of the records is required to piece together your family's role in the pageant of English history than to write a fine tale of the deeds of princes or cabinet committees, to analyse the role of women in the Board of Trade or count the number of millionaires in nineteenth-century Bradford.

The range of records described in this guide is vast (even though it is only a little book); I have only shown the tip of the iceberg, partly for fear of scaring you off! You may have to tussle with strange legal terminology and the most bizarre of filing systems, read unfamiliar handwriting and grasp administrative arrangements as silly as anything in *Gulliver's Travels*. None of this can be done in a day, a week, a month. You will have to keep coming, gently easing yourself into the ways of the PRO and its treasure house of papers, parchments, files and registers. Stick at it and your reward will be immense.

BIBLIOGRAPHY

Books and guides to the records in the PRO have been referred to in the appropriate part of the text.

This list could be endless, as it is it is a personal and idiosyncratic note of books (apart from those mentioned in the text) which I have found especially useful for reference or for conjuring up the past.

Manuals and general guides

C R Cheney (ed), *Handbook of Dates*, Royal Historical Society, 1970.

A J Camp, *My Ancestor was a Migrant*, Society of Genealogists, 1987 (very good on chasing ancestors round the country).

Stella Colwell, *Dictionary of Genealogical Sources in the Public Record Office*, Weidenfeld & Nicolson, 1992.

T V H Fitzhugh, *The Dictionary of Genealogy*, 4th ed, revision by Susan Lumas for the Society of Genealogists, London, 1994.

David Hawgood, *Computers in Family History*, 5th ed, the author, 1994.

George Pelling, *Beginning your Family History*, FFHS, 6th ed, 1995.

Sir F M Powicke and E B Fryde, *Handbook of British Chronology*, Royal Historical Society, 1961.

Pauline Saul, *The Family Historian's Enquire Within*, FFHS, 6th ed, 1995.

Journals

As Family History is growing apace and new sources are being explored and new indexes and compilations are appearing almost daily, it is a good idea to keep abreast of things by means of the genealogical journals. Most family history societies publish their own; you can get a list of societies and their publications from The Federation of Family History Societies (address below).

The national journals are:

Family History News and Digest (the journal of the Federation of Family History Societies).

Family History Monthly, from 1996.

Family Tree Magazine.

Practical Family History, monthly from May 1997.

Genealogists' Magazine.

Background

To my mind the best book for understanding pre-industrial society is *The World we have lost*, Peter Laslett, 2nd ed London, 1971. Take that, and a clutch of traditional nursery rhymes, and you will be making a good fist at imagining how our ancestors conducted themselves from day to day.

Ben Jonson's plays are better than Shakespeare's for depicting sixteenth/early seventeenth-century urban living in the raw. For getting the measure of later seventeenth-century society you cannot do better than *The History of Myddle* and the Restoration comedies. For the eighteenth century you have Daniel Defoe, and Jane Austen for the early nineteenth. Charles Dickens will do splendidly for the next few decades; *Bleak House* will help you feel (if not understand) the workings of the legal system (especially Chancery). Nicholas Rodger's book *The Wooden World* is an admirable entrée to the eighteenth-century Navy and for later seafaring ancestors there are the novels of Joseph Conrad.

And finally, if you have Bethnal Green ancestry (as many of us do at some stage) may I recommend my own book, *London's East End*, London, 1994.

USEFUL ADDRESSES

Addresses specific to various areas of research have been referred to in the appropriate part of the text.

Family Records Centre, 1 Myddelton Street, London EC1 1UW; tel: 0181 392 5300.

Federation of Family History Societies (FFHS), Administrator c/o The Benson Room, Birmingham and Midland Institute, Margaret Street, Birmingham BS 3BS. Publications: 2-4 Killer Street, Ramsbottom, Bury, Lancs BL0 9BZ.

General Register Office, Office of National Statistics, Postal Application Section, Smedley Hydro, Trafalgar Road, Birkdale, Southport PR8 2HH.

Institute of Heraldic and Genealogical Studies, Northgate, Canterbury, Kent CT1 1BA; tel: 01227 68664.

Royal Commission on Historical Manuscripts and National Register of Archives, Quality House, Quality Court, Chancery Lane, London WC2A 1HP; tel: 0171 242 1198.

Society of Genealogists, 14 Charterhouse Buildings, Goswell Road, London EC1M 7BA; tel: 0171 251 8799.